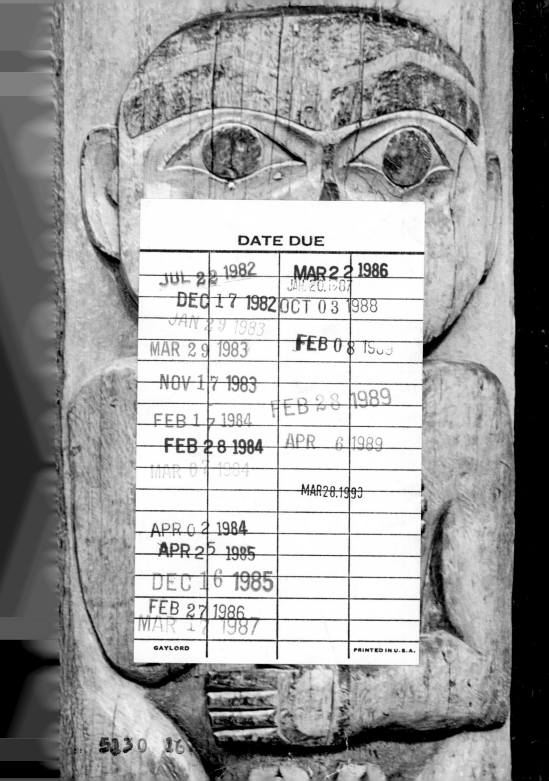

SOUTHEAST
Alaska's Panhandle

Volume 5, Number 2, 1978

Introduction 4
Land, Forest, Sea, Growth and Economy,
People, Communities

Ketchikan & Vicinity 33
Saxman, Metlakatla, Hyder, Myers Chuck

Prince of Wales Island 61
Klawock, Craig, Hydaburg, Thorne Bay,
Kasaan, Point Baker, Port Protection

Wrangell, Petersburg & Vicinity 81
Kupreanof, Kake

Sitka & Vicinity 103
Port Alexander, Tenakee Springs, Hoonah,
Pelican, Elfin Cove

Juneau & Vicinity 135
Admiralty Island, Angoon

Glacier Bay, Haines, Skagway 160
Gustavus, Lynn Canal

Northern Panhandle, Yakutat 180
Lituya Bay, Icy Bay

Southeastern Facts & Figures 188
Largest islands, community populations,
weather, dates in history

ALASKA GEOGRAPHIC.

The Alaska Geographic Society

To teach many more to better know and use our natural resources

About This Issue:

Patricia Roppel, photographed in Ketchikan by Lael Morgan, Staff

The Alaska Geographic Society's staff editors began work on this edition more than two years ago by collecting photographs of Southeastern Alaska — first hundreds, then literally thousands — from readers, residents, working photographers . . . anyone who might have something to contribute. Then came the matter of text — we had access to a profusion of background information on Southeastern, but who would pull the pieces together and write a manuscript? The decision was easy enough — we asked Patricia Roppel, and she accepted the assignment. (Pat is a Southeastern resident, a regular contributor to *The ALASKA JOURNAL®* and a determined researcher. Last year Pàt was named Historian of the Year by the Alaska Historical Society.) She writes for two publications in her hometown, Ketchikan, *The New Alaskan* and *The Southeast Log*, and also has taken on a few writing assignments for the Alaska Department of Fish & Game. She and her husband, Frank, have two children and a boat, and not long ago took up scuba diving.

Editors: Robert A. Henning, Marty Loken, Barbara Olds, Lael Morgan, Robert N. De Armond
Designer: Roselyn Pape
Cartographer: Jon.Hersh

THE ALASKA GEOGRAPHIC SOCIETY is a nonprofit organization exploring new frontiers of knowledge across the lands of the polar rim, learning how other men and other countries live in their Norths, putting the geography book back in the classroom, exploring new methods of teaching and learning—sharing in the excitement of discovery in man's wonderful new world north of 51°16'.

MEMBERS OF THE SOCIETY RECEIVE *Alaska Geographic®*, a quality magazine in color which devotes each quarterly issue to monographic in-depth coverage of a northern geographic region or resource-oriented subject.

MEMBERSHIP DUES in The Alaska Geographic Society are $20 for initiation and the first year, $16 thereafter. (Eighty percent of the first year's dues is for a one-year subscription to *Alaska Geographic®*.) Order from The Alaska Geographic Society, Box 4-EEE, Anchorage, Alaska 99509; (907) 243-1484.

MATERIAL SOUGHT: The editors of *Alaska Geographic®* seek a wide variety of informative material on the lands north of 51°16' on geographic subjects—anything to do with resources and their uses (with heavy emphasis on

quality color photography)—from Alaska, Northern Canada, Siberia, Japan—all geographic areas that have a relationship to Alaska in a physical or economic sense. (In mid-1978 editors were seeking photographs and other materials on the following subjects: Stikine River drainage; Yukon-Kuskokwim Delta region; shellfish and shellfisheries of Alaska; Aleutian Islands; Wrangell and Saint Elias Mountains, and Alaska's Great Interior.) We do not want material done in excessive scientific terminology. A query to the editors is suggested. Payments are made for all material upon publication.

CHANGE OF ADDRESS: The post office does not automatically forward *Alaska Geographic®* when you move. To insure continuous service, notify us six weeks before moving. Send us your new address and zip code (and moving date), your old address and zip code, and if possible send a mailing label from a copy of *Alaska Geographic®*. Send this information to *Alaska Geographic®* Mailing Offices, 130 Second Avenue South, Edmonds, Washington 98020.

Second-class postage paid at Edmonds, Washington 98020. Printed in U.S.A.

Trademark: *Alaska Geographic*. Library of Congress catalog card number 72-92087.
ISSN 0361-1353; key title *Alaska Geographic*.
ISBN 0-88240-107-6.

Cover photo — **A view across Wrangell Narrows from Petersburg to the waterfront community of Kupreanof (formerly West Petersburg), on Kupreanof Island. (Richard Billings)**
Overleaf — **A totemic face at Sitka National Historical Monument. (Dan Kowalski)**
Left — **Layers of mountain ridges at the north end of Baranof Island. (Stephen Hilson)**

INTRODUCTION

Southeastern Alaska is that seemingly insignificant little scraggly piece of real estate hanging on precariously to the lower right-hand corner of the big Alaska map. Its narrowed coastline, where the great Fairweather Range bulges out from the Canadian hinterlands to the waters of the North Pacific, seems barely enough to keep this scrap of land tied to the bigger Alaska land mass to the north and west. Yet this is the land where for most of Alaska's young history the greater bulk of the population once lived. This is where Russians built a city that was termed by some the "capital of the Pacific," a headquarters operation for all Russian endeavors in the east Pacific regions, and where English and Spanish and French and Yankees explored and left their names behind. This is where the first of Alaska's great salmon canneries were built. Here were some of the largest and richest gold mines in the world. Here also was the homeland of Tlingits, some Haidas, and a few late-arriving Tsimshians. And before them, unknown people who only left a few notes of their passing scribed in stone at the mouths of rivers and just beyond the tide.

Southeastern is a sea and mountain world with islands and islands, bays, channels, vast sounds, great gashes of deep fjords, glaciers spilling down from endless ice fields and calving fantasyland blue and white bergs. A green, green land — a dozen varying shades of green — in waters and trees and meadows and ice. Quiet. Miles and miles of roadless unpopulated beaches mostly unmarked by man, new marks rare, old marks barely discernible.

The occasional clearcuts of loggers, the falling in ruins of old canneries, here and there a small fishing camp, a larger Native village, transitory things in this wild and sparsely settled land where junglelike growth in the wet and mild climate soon blurs or obliterates the marks of man's passing. Steering a boat at night up and down the long passages, hours can pass without a light, perhaps only the stars overhead, the phosphorescent dartings of fish before the bow, and with engines off maybe a soft cry of a passing bird in the velvet of the dark, a humpback whale singing its strange songlike sound across the waters. A still land, empty, but alive and ageless.

Leaping fish, always working white gulls, and white-headed bald

4

Peaks above Starrigavan Bay, on the west coast of Baranof Island, 5.5 miles north of Sitka. (Ed Cooper)

eagles dotting the treelined shores like scattered popcorn. Great brown bears roaming the tide flats for roots, for grass, for salmon. And on other islands where the brown bears disdain, black bears. And on most all the islands the delicate small Sitka blacktail deer, high in the alpine meadows in summer, crowded in the deep snows of winter down to the scant browse along the shore.

The canneries are all but gone, the capital at Juneau is slated to be moved, the population shift has moved the epicenter of government "to the Westward" as Southeastern Alaskans of yesteryears used to refer to the Anchorage area, and mining is a forgotten industry. But the number of people here continues to increase as elsewhere in the world, and government has grown apace. Property is higher, harder to buy, and government and pulp have replaced fishing and mines for industrial backbone, but the deep beauty of the land reminds that the state's number two industry is tourism and in Southeastern Alaska tourism is big. Although only one in twenty in a recent survey in Anchorage and Fairbanks had ever seen Southeastern Alaska (they fly over or drive around), the people of the tourist world know this land, its protected sea lanes, its Indian totems and glaciers, its timeless loveliness. Closer to "the States," more bountifully blessed with natural beauties than the farther west and farther north parts of Alaska, though facing the loss of capital city workers and mines and canneries, the people of the Panhandle take pride in calling their home "the banana belt." Here it doesn't get as cold, the sun remains higher in the winter months, hangs almost as long in the sky in summer, and peeks often enough through frequent rain clouds to cause the loyal to declare, "When the sun shines it's the most beautiful place on earth."

From our window in our Southeastern Alaska home we watch 5-hour sunsets, pods of humpback whales feeding on great schools of herring, gulls, scoters, mergansers, cormorants, mallards, loons, chickadees, red-headed sapsuckers, olive-backed hummingbirds and their occasional friends the ruby-throats. Crows chase away the bigger ravens and both chase away the eagles. Now and then a small fishing boat goes by, making waves that become smaller and smaller and eventually die away. The current of the tide moves gently by in most places, fiercely over the reefs as the waters of the bay rush to the

There is no such thing as "iceberg blue" — they come in all ranges of blue and white, with colors sometimes intensifying under overcast skies. (Pete Martin)

straits outside as nature speeds to keep her 6-hour turnaround schedule of low to high, high to low, from minus 4 feet to plus 18 twice a day.

The air is sweet. There is a soft aroma of spruce and berries and other things. Man makes little sounds quickly swallowed. Someone wrote in our guest book the most descriptive line — "Peace."

Still Tlingit country. The Russians didn't stay, didn't master it. And where the metropolitan white man has since built a handful of small communities along the shore, the eagles still soar above the streets, there is yet green forest and mountain on every hand. An airport or two with rushing jets, a freeway or two with bumper-to-bumper cars at quitting time haven't seemed to change this land.

We said recently that Cook Inlet country was "where the action is." Of Southeastern we won't go so far as to say "this is where the action ain't," but if that is to a certain extent true, many of us Southeasterners like it that way. In an otherwise hustling, bustling world of chase-the-buck, here we have, as the friend declared in our guest book — "Peace." And a land of infinite beauty.

Robert A. Henning

5

We do have our wet times
and our cold times,
but even then there is a
natural beauty that insists on
manifesting itself.
Rain in a big and dirty city can
be a dreary thing. Here, it is a
fiercely beautiful thing of clouds
torn to shreds in a gale
or a gossamer thing of gentle mists
sifting past the dripping eaves
and drifting softly through
the spruce.

— "MAIN TRAILS & BYPATHS®"
THE ALASKA SPORTSMAN®, August 1960,
describing Southeastern Alaska

Fog over the north arm of Dundas Bay, in Glacier Bay National
Monument. (William Boehm)

Left — Southeastern is a place where virtually all towns and villages face the
water . . . whether ocean, quiet fjord or river. This scene is at Sitka — fishing boats,
weathered houses and reflections — but it could have been taken in many
Southeastern towns. (Tim Thompson)
Above — An old homestead at Amalga Harbor, 19 miles northwest of Juneau,
photographed in November. (Eric Bailey)

Below — Southeastern's back country offers tremendous recreation potential for residents and increasing numbers of visitors. This camper has kayaked into Muir Inlet, in Glacier Bay National Monument, to soak up the silence. (Tom Bean)
Right — Fall colors and fresh snow along the Chilkat River north of Haines. (John Helle)

THE LAND

S ome 10,000 years ago, Southeastern Alaska emerged from the last great ice age as a glacially sculptured landscape. What was once covered by masses of ice has evolved into a fertile and scenic blend of mountains, forest and water.

This unique region is the storied Panhandle of the southern part of Alaska, known for its striking beauty, abundant wildlife, varied ethnologic groups and rich historical heritage.

Southeastern is both a narrow and rugged strip of seaboard along the west side of the mighty Coast Mountains, and a maze of 1,000-plus islands strung immediately offshore from the mainland. It extends from Dixon Entrance on the south to Icy Bay and Mount Saint Elias on the north. The international boundary, whose southern line is formed by Portland Canal, runs its jagged northern course along the irregular aggregate of peaks in the Coast Mountains.

At the northern end of Southeastern Alaska is the Fairweather Range, part of the Saint Elias Mountains—highest coastal mountains in the world. Between Mount Fairweather (15,300 feet) and Mount Saint Elias (18,008 feet) the international boundary follows the crest of the chain at an average distance of only 30 miles from the coast. Along this stretch of the boundary are other impressive pinnacles, such as Mount Vancouver (15,700 feet), Mount Augusta (14,070 feet) and Mount Root (12,860 feet).

A massive icecap covers much of these mountain ranges, and large glaciers funnel down valleys from the high reaches. Some of these glaciers extend to the heads of fjords, where they discharge great icebergs into the sea. Other glaciers descend only part way, and milky, silt-laden rivers carry the meltwater through intricate channels to the sea.

The Coast Mountains of the mainland, viewed from Frederick Sound, north of Petersburg. (Joe Upton)

One of the largest ice masses on the North American continent, Malaspina Glacier, is in the northwestern extremity of the region. In the shadow of the lofty Fairweather Range, Glacier Bay offers some of Alaska's most magnificent glacial scenery. Numerous great tongues of ice push their way to the sea, where icebergs crack off near-vertical ice cliffs and plummet into the water. The bergs drift until grounded or until they disintegrate in the warmer water and summer air.

Farther south in the Coast Mountains, Dawes Glacier in Endicott Arm and the two Sawyer glaciers in Tracy Arm calve giant, green and blue icebergs into Holkham Bay, an extensive inlet that indents the Coast Mountains not far from Juneau. The only Southeastern glacier accessible by road is Mendenhall, near Juneau. Its crevasses and caverns, reflecting iridescent blue, end in a lake made of the glacier's meltwater.

Great trenches indent the mainland where glaciers once pushed to the sea. Today they are spectacular fjords with steep slopes rising from the water's edge to alplike peaks.

Thousands of rivers and streams course down the mountains and through the valleys. Major rivers originate in Canada: the Alsek, Chilkat, Taku, Whiting, Stikine and Unuk. (Of these rivers which traverse the Pacific Mountain system, only the Stikine is considered navigable.) Other large rivers are the Klehini, Chickamin, Bradfield, Speel and Taiya. Many spring directly from glaciers, and the milky waters can be seen mixing with the clear ocean waters as the river joins the sea.

Offshore from these mainland mountains, glaciers and rivers is the Alexander Archipelago—hundreds of islands covered with dark-green forests of spruce, hemlock and cedar. These islands are separated by sounds, straits, channels and narrows. Many of the seaways are deep: Chatham Strait, the major waterway bisecting the Alexander Archipelago, attains depths of 2,000 feet, while many of the other fjords reach depths of 400 feet. These waterways provide a water route through Southeastern—the famed Inside Passage—where watercraft, from canoes to ships, can travel in relatively protected waters, thus avoiding the often turbulent, open Pacific.

The combination of mountains and the nearby ocean insures a climate dominated by maritime weather. Warmed by ocean currents, Southeastern experiences mild summers, with temperatures averaging about 60°F. Occasional readings in the high eighties are recorded, but bright, clear days are the exception. (The Japan Current, about 40 miles offshore from Southeastern's outer islands, occasionally moves closer to shore, causing temperature changes and carrying with it unusual tropical fish.)

Winters are cool, but not severely cold, with alternating snow, rain and sunshine. Sub-zero temperatures are uncommon, and thermometers often hover in the mid-thirties.

Long, incessant rains and drizzles are characteristic, but storms and heavier rainfall can occur year-round. Storms are most frequent and precipitation is heaviest from November through January. Average precipitation is more than 100 inches in much of this region, ranging from 26 inches in Skagway to more than 221 inches at Little Port Walter on Baranof Island.

Winter snows generally melt after a few days at lower elevations in the southern third of the area. In the mountains and around glaciers, more than 200 inches of snow is recorded each year, perpetuating the glaciers.

Grounded icebergs in Goose Cove, on the east shore of Muir Inlet in Glacier Bay National Monument. (Michael Nigro)

THE FOREST

Southeastern's cool, moist conditions have produced a lush forest, which is an extension of the rainbelt forests of the Pacific Northwest. Designated Tongass National Forest in 1907, this vast greenbelt contains more than 73% of the land in Southeastern Alaska.

The treeline usually extends from sea level to about 3,000 feet in the southern part of the region and to 1,800 feet farther north, in the Icy Strait region. In the south the forests are primarily western hemlock and Sitka spruce, with scattered red cedar and Alaska yellow cedar. In the north the percentage of hemlock increases and mountain hemlock becomes important. Red cedar extends only to the northern shore of Frederick Sound, and Alaska yellow cedar is often found only as a small tree in swamps or muskegs.

Other common species are red alder, found along streams, on landslides and other highly disturbed areas; black cottonwood, seen in major mainland river valleys; and lodgepole pine.

Beneath the towering conifers of the coastal forest are flourishing young evergreens and shrubs, such as devil's club, blueberry, huckleberry, and rusty manziesia. Moss and ferns cover the ground, and lichens drape many trees.

Opposite page — **Mosses, ferns and other shade-loving plants cover the rain forest floor in Southeastern Alaska. Prominent trees in Southeastern are western hemlock, which forms about 73% of the dense coastal forests; Sitka spruce, which comprises more than 20% of the region's forests, and red cedar, Alaska yellow cedar, red alder, black cottonwood and lodgepole pine. (Pete Martin)**
Left — **Branches from common trees and bushes found in Southeastern. From left to right, top row — alder, dogwood; center row — western hemlock, Sitka spruce, cedar; bottom row — blueberry, willow. (Roger Hoff, reprinted from** *ALASKA*® **magazine)**

Clockwise from above, this page — **A killer whale and its young in Glacier Bay National Monument. (William Boehm) / A black bear in brown color phase, photographed in Glacier Bay National Monument. (Tom Bean) / Mountain goats often are seen in the high places of Southeastern; this animal was photographed on Mount Wright, at the entrance to Muir Inlet in Glacier Bay National Monument. (William Boehm) / A bald eagle at Porter Cove, on the mainland north of Petersburg. Southeastern Alaska has the world's greatest concentration of eagles, especially on Admiralty Island. (Richard Billings)**

18

The dense forest is broken by muskeg bogs, glacial outwash plains and marshlands in river valleys and deltas, and wild flowers splash color against a varied green background. In addition to the mature coniferous forest, these open areas—the streams, rocky ridges and other features—provide variations in vegetation necessary for wildlife to proliferate.

Sitka blacktail deer spend much of their time in the coastal forest where the dense and rank undergrowth provides a shield against enemies, including its two chief predators, the wolf and the bear. Wolves are common on the mainland and most of the islands, except Baranof, Chichagof and Admiralty. Black bears, the most abundant and widely distributed species in Southeastern, are found throughout the forested region, except on Admiralty, Baranof and Chichagof Islands. It is on these three islands, plus the mainland, that the enormous, sometimes fierce, brown, or grizzly, bear wanders feeding on a mixture of plant life and meat. The blue, or glacier, bear (a color phase of the black bear) is seen infrequently near Yakutat.

Mountain goat transplants have been established on Baranof Island in recent years, but the alpine zone of the mainland is their natural home, and it supports some of the largest goat populations in North

Clockwise from left — **Fog, trees and devil's club undergrowth on Douglas Island, near Juneau. (Tim Thompson) / Wolves live in most areas of Southeastern Alaska, but are not often photographed because of the region's lack of open country. (William Boehm) /Nagoonberries at Gustavus, near the boundary of Glacier Bay National Monument. (David Nemeth)**

Clockwise from right, this page — **The crow is a common sight in Southeastern. This one is working over a salmon scrap in Petersburg. (James Mackovjak) / Red (sockeye) salmon head for the spawning grounds in a Southeastern Alaska stream. (Lou Barr, National Marine Fisheries Service) / Sitka blacktail fawn on Admiralty Island. (Stan Price)**

20

America. Far above timber line, they browse alpine meadows traversing steep, rocky outcrops as they migrate in search of food. Elk were transplanted to Kruzof Island in the early 1920's, but have not been reported in the past 30 years. Moose are not prolific and occur only in the larger river drainages and in the Yakutat Foreland.

A limited number of lynx, wolverines, foxes, mink and land otters range widely through the area. Shrews, red squirrels, brown bats, flying squirrels, deer mice, red-backed voles, porcupines and pine marten are typically of the forest and are not often found away from it.

Blue grouse, great horned owls, woodpeckers, Steller's jays and thrushes are some of the primary birds within the forests. Robins, fox sparrows, hummingbirds and swallows can be heard and seen along the forest edge. More bald eagles live in Southeastern Alaska than in any other place in the world. They nest in the forest but frequent the tidelands, which provide most of their food.

Clockwise from left — **Three popular fish in Southeastern Alaska, from top to bottom: silver (coho) salmon, pink (humpback) salmon, and red (sockeye) salmon. (Mike Jobanek, reprinted from *The MILEPOST®*) / Harbor seals on ice in Muir Inlet, Glacier Bay National Monument. (Tom Bean) / One of the most popular crab species in Southeastern is the Dungeness, trapped or "dug" in shallow waters with shovels, oars or other handy implements. (Richard Billings)**

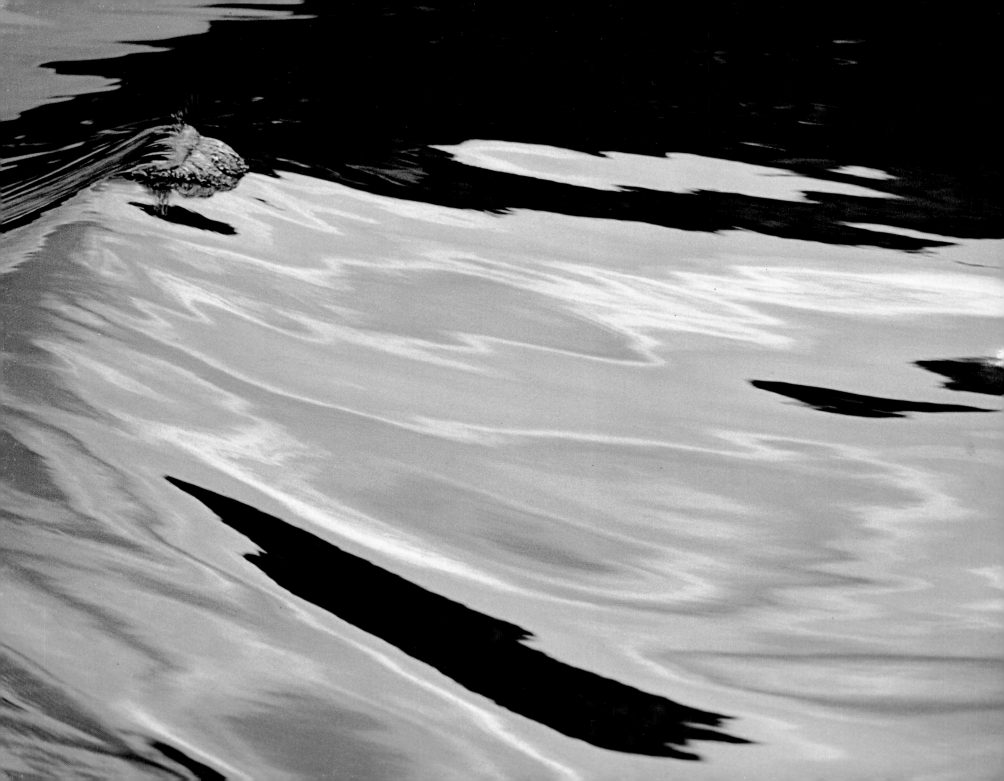

THE SEA

Often only a step away from the forest is the sea. The ocean and the complex coastlines, with their rocky intertidal areas, mud flats, and sandy beaches, are home to many species of invertebrates, fish, birds and mammals. The tide rises and falls twice daily with an extreme range from minus 4 feet to plus 18 feet—a difference of 22 feet. This rising and falling of the tide circulates and mixes marine waters, providing an abundant food source for the marine life.

Common among the invertebrates are Dungeness, tanner and king crab, shrimp, butter clams, sea urchins and sea cucumbers. Crab and shrimp are caught commercially and processed by freezing and canning.

The ocean waters teem with fish—most significant being the five species of Pacific salmon: sockeye, chum, king, coho and pink. Each year during the summer and fall, the salmon return to the thousands of streams and rivers to spawn, and many are intercepted by fishermen. During 1970-74, Southeastern salmon harvests accounted for 38% of the total Alaskan harvest.

Commercial harvests are also made on herring, halibut and sablefish (black cod). Foreign fleets along the continental shelf edge and slope traditionally have sought Pacific perch, walleye pollack and flatfish. With extended jurisdiction (in 1977 the United States extended its fishing limit to 200 miles offshore), Alaskans are developing plans for a bottom fishery to utilize these species formerly caught by foreign fleets.

Several species of cetaceans, particularly Dall and harbor porpoises and humpback, fin and Pacific killer whales, are common in Southeastern waters. Gray whales and the northern fur seal pass offshore during migration, and the elephant seal has been recorded on occasion.

Large numbers of waterfowl, such as diving ducks, mallards, mergansers and Canada geese, can be seen, and more than 50 species of sea birds, including terns, gulls, kittiwakes, auklets and murres, have been sighted in the coastal waters of the region.

Left — **Wake of the purse seiner** *Alsek*. **(Mary Henrikson)**
Right — **Rivers carry glacial silt and mud to the sea all along the coast of Southeastern Alaska, sometimes creating harsh contrasts such as this one near Wrangell, where the Stikine River reaches tidewater. (Nicholas Wheeler)**

24

Southeastern Alaska has some of the state's most powerful tiderips, where huge volumes of water are compressed through narrow channels between islands and in the entrances to many bays. This sequence of photographs dramatically illustrates what happens when the tide begins to run in Sergius Narrows, on the north side of Baranof Island. Pull of the tide increases until the large anchored buoy (not the easiest thing to submerge) is pulled completely underwater.

Left — A seine skiff works against the tide in Secluded Bay, on the west coast of Baranof Island. (Both by Robert E. Johnson)

25

GROWTH AND ECONOMY

N atural resources traditionally have been the mainstay of the economy of Southeastern, principally marine resources, minerals and forest products.

In the early American period, the fur trade remained as the main economic interest, but the numbers of fur-bearing animals continued to diminish. It was salmon that attracted entrepreneurs and renewed interest in the land known as Seward's Folly. Salmon were present in such large numbers that it was rumored streams could be crossed by walking on their backs.

Numerous canneries sprung up after the first were established at Klawock and Old Sitka in 1878. The size of the salmon pack rapidly increased until it peaked in the late 1930's, when runs began to decline. But fishing continues to provide a traditional way of life, and fishing villages are still significant in coastal areas and may become more so now that the State of Alaska and several nonprofit aquaculture corporations have entered into salmon-enhancement programs.

Of all the Southeastern resources, minerals historically have held the spotlight. It was the magic word *gold* that brought the first surge of pioneers after the purchase of Alaska. Twenty years before the influx of the 98ers of the Klondike gold rush, the first full-fledged gold mining camp, Shuck Camp, was established near Windham Bay. More stimulation to mining in the region came when gold was discovered in the Cassiar District of British Columbia in the 1870's, and the Stikine River became a popular route to these gold fields. Prospectors spread from the Stikine and Cassiar districts into the Alexander Archipelago and the neighboring mainland.

Gold was discovered in 1880 at what is now Juneau, and in 1881 at Douglas. With this concentration of activities and the resulting increase in population, the territorial capital was moved from Sitka to Juneau in 1906. Southeastern was on its way to becoming the dominant region of Alaska. It held this position until the Second World War, when military activity and the Alaska Highway shifted emphasis to Anchorage and Fairbanks.

The war also brought major gold operations to a halt, and for all

Left — **Fur, fish, minerals and timber have created several booms in Southeastern Alaska . . . and left many buildings such as this long-abandoned store at Killisnoo. (Joe Upton)**
Right — **A small part of Ketchikan's seine fleet ties up at the New England Fish Company dock. (Ken Elverum)**

Clockwise from right, this page — The timber industry has emerged in the past two decades as a major economic factor in Southeastern. Cants (fairly large-dimension timbers) await loading for shipment from Wrangell to Japan, where they will be sawn into smaller-dimension lumber. (Tim Thompson) / Hank Nelson cuts a large hemlock on Wrangell Island. (Charlotte Casey) / Lumber is stacked at a mill in Wrangell. (Tim Thompson)

practical purposes mining has been dead in the region since 1944. Gold is not the only valuable mineral hidden beneath the mountains. Copper, lead, silver, zinc, palladium and building stones such as limestone, gypsum and marble have been mined. Some plans for renewal of mining activities are afoot. A molybdenum deposit near Ketchikan, a nickel deposit on Yakobi Island and/or the iron at Klukwan and Snettisham may eventually add to Alaska's economy. Exploration is also continuing in the Gulf Coast petroleum fields near Yakutat.

The basic economy in Southeastern began to shift at midcentury with the development of forest products industries. Pulp mills at Ketchikan and Sitka went into operation. Sawmills were expanded or built to export cants to Japan and lumber to domestic markets in the continental United States. Logging camps were built at remote sites to provide the necessary timber and nearly 60 of them are still in operation.

The recent growth of the state and local government has provided major sources of employment and stimulated development of retail trade, transportation, services and construction.

Tourism and recreation are major components of the region's economy. The glaciers, mountains, sheltered waterways, wild lands and fish and wildlife populations provide recreational opportunities which often cannot be experienced elsewhere in the United States. Trails from salt water to inland lakes and along rivers and streams and nearly 150 U.S. Forest Service cabins on lakes, provide access to

THE SOUTHEASTERN ALASKA MARINE HIGHWAY FLEET
(All except the newest addition, the *Aurora*, which is nearly identical to the *LeConte*.)

Columbia (418 feet, 1,000 passengers)

Malaspina (408 feet, 750 passengers)

Taku (352 feet, 500 passengers)

Matanuska (352 feet, 500 passengers)

LeConte (235 feet, 250 passengers)

Chilkat (99 feet, 75 passengers)

(Photos courtesy of Division of Tourism, reprinted from *The MILEPOST®*)

Cruise ships bring thousands of visitors to Southeastern Alaska each summer. Tourists aboard the S.S. *Fairsea* enjoy a sunny day at Glacier Bay National Monument. (Tom Bean)

cutthroat, rainbow, Dolly Varden, steelhead and other species. Boating on the many sheltered waterways, beachcombing, fishing, hunting, camping, hiking and photography account for most leisure-time activities.

Most of the region's towns, situated on islands or the narrow coastal plain, lack connecting roads and must be reached by ship or airplane. State ferries transport people and vehicles between most major Southeastern ports and to Prince Rupert, British Columbia, and Seattle, Washington. At Haines, Alaska, they connect with the Haines Highway, which is linked to the Alaska Highway and offers a direct overland route to Interior and Southcentral Alaska . . . as well as through Canada.

Another jumping-off point at the northern end of the Inside Passage is Skagway, where ferries and cruise ships connect with the White Pass & Yukon Route narrow-gauge railroad to Whitehorse, Yukon Territory, and with the new Skagway-Carcross Road, due for completion in 1978. The road will offer connections with the Alaska Highway near Whitehorse.

Cruise ships bring thousands of visitors to view the rocky and wooded islands along the fjorded coast and to spend a few hours in major ports. But it is the airplane that plays the vital role in transportation. Landing strips and/or seaplane facilities are available at virtually all communities, and at most logging camps and canneries.

29

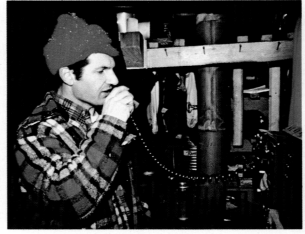

Clockwise from above — **Jim Greenough, sometimes clinical psychologist, works at his other job — commercial hand-trolling — aboard his sailboat, *Windflower*. It might be safe to say that Greenough, of Sitka, is the *only* psychologist using a sailboat for a troller in Southeastern. (Tim Thompson) / The Ga Ja Heen Dancers (Tlingit) perform at Sitka. Other well-known dance groups in Southeastern include the Chilkat Dancers of Haines, and the New Archangel Dancers (Russian) of Sitka. (James Simmen) / A. M. Johnson, a prospector from Ketchikan. (Dan Kowalski) / John Lepore, of Game Creek, a small Christian farming community on Chichagof Island, uses the CB radio to talk with friends at Hoonah, about 5 miles away by water. (Marty Loken, Staff)**

PEOPLE, COMMUNITIES

A feeling of vastness, wilderness and solitude is imparted and reinforced by the low-population density. More than 95% of the land in Southeastern is under federal jurisdiction; the Tongass National Forest alone accounts for more than 73% of the region's total area. As a result, land ownership is less complicated in Southeastern than in most regions of the state. However, many of the withdrawals will terminate and ownerships will change during the next several years because of selection authorizations to Native corporations resulting from the Alaska Native Claims Settlement Act; claims by the state under the Statehood Act; and with the resolution of the issue of national-interest lands by Congress.

Little of the land is occupied. In 1977 an estimated 47,500 people lived in the Southeastern region. Urbanization has proceeded rapidly and more than three-fourths of the population live in the five major urban areas of Juneau, Ketchikan, Petersburg, Sitka and Wrangell. Most of the others live in 25 smaller communities, each averaging less than 500 people, with some as small as Kasaan, 33, and Kupreanof, 42.

Many of the Tlingit, Haida and Tsimshian people live in urban Southeastern. Others have chosen to live in their traditional villages of Angoon, Hoonah, Hydaburg, Saxman, Kasaan, Kake, Klawock, Klukwan, Yakutat and Metlakatla.

The majority of the population in Southeastern is concentrated in the central portion of the Panhandle—that area from Sumner Strait north to Icy Strait and the mouth of Lynn Canal. Major cities are Petersburg, Sitka, and Southeastern's largest city, Juneau.

In the southern portion—from Sumner Strait south to the Canadian border—the largest population concentrations are in Ketchikan and Wrangell. The rugged northern portion—which includes Lynn Canal, Glacier Bay and Yakutat Bay—has the smallest population.

The communities of Southeastern Alaska began in a variety of ways. Some were settled before the white man arrived, many attribute their founding to the mighty salmon, and a few can look back to the glitter of gold.

On the following pages, generally from south to north, are profiles of Southeastern's most notable communities and attractions.

A good example of hand-built housing in Southeastern. This place is near the beach at Lena Cove, 14 miles northwest of Juneau. (Bruce Baker)

KETCHIKAN

The Ketchikan area, as defined by the map at right, includes several islands — Revillagigedo, Gravina, Annette and Duke being the largest — and a sizable section of mainland "back country" east of Ketchikan. Included are some of Southeastern Alaska's most impressive fjords; the southernmost being 70-mile-long Portland Canal, which penetrates the coast along the extreme southern border of Alaska and ends at the adjoining towns of Hyder, Alaska, and Stewart, British Columbia. Behm Canal wraps nearly around Revillagigedo Island, stretching 108 miles along the island's eastern, northern and northwestern shores. Other major inlets include Boca de Quadra, Smeaton Bay, Rudyerd Bay, Punchbowl Cove, Walker Cove and Burroughs Bay.

Opposite page — Ketchikan's waterfront is on Tongass Narrows, facing Gravina Island (site of Ketchikan's airport, reached by a small shuttle ferry). Deer Mountain, 3,001 feet, rises behind town. (Terry Schneider)
Inset, opposite page — Overview of Ketchikan, Tongass Narrows and Gravina Island, with the Ketchikan airport visible on the far side of the channel. (Dale Pulju)

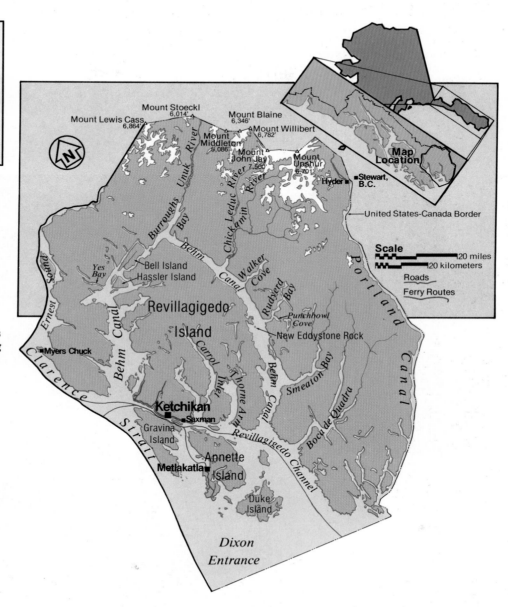

Map Location

United States-Canada Border

Scale
20 miles
20 kilometers
Roads
Ferry Routes

Mount Lewis Cass
8,864'
Mount Stoeckl
6,014'
Mount Blaine
6,346'
Mount Willibert
6,782'
Mount Middleton
9,086'
Mount John Jay
7,500'
Mount Upshur
6,701'
Hyder
Stewart, B.C.

Burroughs Bay
Unuk River
Behm Canal
Leduc River
Chickamin River
Walker Cove
Rudyerd Bay
Punchbowl Cove
New Eddystone Rock

Ernest Sound

Yes Bay
Bell Island
Hassler Island

Revillagigedo Island

Behm Canal

Carrol Inlet
Thorne Arm
Behm Canal
Smeaton Bay
Boca de Quadra

Portland Canal

Myers Chuck

Clarence Strait

Ketchikan
Saxman

Gravina Island

Metlakatla
Annette Island

Revillagigedo Channel

Duke Island

Dixon Entrance

33

Right — The cruise ship *Island Princess* anchors just offshore at Ketchikan, named the "First City" because it is the first stop for many northbound vessels. Some cruise ships have announced they will by-pass the city, but the harbor remains a busy place during the summer season. (Ken Elverum)
Lower right — Another rainy night in Ketchikan. (William Boehm)
Lower left — Ketchikan boasts the "Tallest Barometer in the World," a liquid-sunshine gauge that keeps track of the town's rainfall. Precipitation averages 154 inches per year. (Lael Morgan, Staff)

34

Clinging to steep hillsides along Tongass Narrows is Ketchikan, the "First City," so nicknamed because it is the first port of entry into Southeastern Alaska for vessels sailing the Inside Passage. It is a linear waterfront city with much of its business district suspended on pilings above the water, and many of its homes perched on cliffs and reached by wooden stairways or narrow, winding board streets. Over the years the business district has stretched out, earning the town the description of being 5 miles long and two blocks wide. City and borough population was 11,490 in 1977, making Ketchikan the state's fourth-largest city, behind Anchorage, Fairbanks and Juneau.

The waterfront is a scene of constant activity and sounds: the deafening buzz of a departing floatplane, the quieter boats, the hum of tugs pulling gigantic barges piled high with cargo for points north, and often overhead the scream of gulls and the graceful gliding of a bald eagle.

Through the waters in front of the town pass cargo tugs, lumber carriers and passenger ships, all sustaining Ketchikan's economy. The same waters are a thoroughfare for fishing boats, which have, since Ketchikan's early days, added to the town's role as a major Alaska fishing port.

Many homes cling to Ketchikan's steep hillsides, and are reached by stairway-streets. This view is down the stairs along Edmonds Street, with Thomas Basin in the background. (Ken Elverum)

35

Southeastern Alaska's huge fishing industry grew to its peak in the Ketchikan area. The town became known as the Salmon Capital of the World and 11 canneries operated in town and at nearby Ward Cove and George Inlet. Some years during the 1930's more than 1.5 million cases of salmon were packed in Ketchikan.

Ketchikan remains an active fishing center and headquarters for a large fleet, but today, with the decline in fish runs, only two canneries continue to pack salmon: Ward Cove Packing Company, which has the distinction of having canned salmon every season since its founding in 1912—except in 1971, when no fish were packed in Ketchikan—and the jointly operated Whitney-Fidalgo Seafoods, Inc.-New England Fish Company cannery.

Canning is not the only method for preserving fish, and freezing at a cold storage also has become a thriving business. Fishing vessels unload halibut, herring and salmon at the docks of

Upper left — **Fishing supplies and other outdoor gear . . . a typical storefront scene in Ketchikan. (Dan Kowalski)**
Above — **Crew members of the seiner** *Middleton* **offload salmon to a tender boat near Ketchikan.**
Left — **The salmon is king in the Southeastern Alaska fishing business, and Ketchikan is one of the region's most active fishing ports. (Both by Tim Thompson)**
Right — **The deck crew of the purse seiner** *Redoubt* **hauls in the gear while the skiff man holds the net away from the boat. Some of Southeastern Alaska's most successful seine boats are based in Ketchikan. (Chip Porter)**

36

New England Fish Company and E. C. Phillips and Son. The frozen seafood is shipped to market in freezer vans aboard barges or the Alaska state ferries.

Fishing, as a basic economy, now shares the stage with harvest of another renewable resource—timber. In the heart of downtown Ketchikan stands Alaska's oldest continuously operated manufacturing industry, Ketchikan Spruce Mills, founded in 1903. North of Ketchikan, across the cove from Ward Cove Packing Company is Ketchikan Pulp Company, recently renamed Louisiana Pacific, Ketchikan Division. Giant log rafts are moored in the cove and often are seen being towed along the narrow waterways from one of 26 logging camps in the vicinity.

The timber industry is important in Southeastern Alaska, especially in Ketchikan. Timber is loaded aboard a freighter at the Ketchikan Spruce Mills dock; some timber is shipped to the Pacific Northwest, but most, in the form of cants, goes to Japan where it is milled into small-dimension lumber. (Dan Kowalski)

38

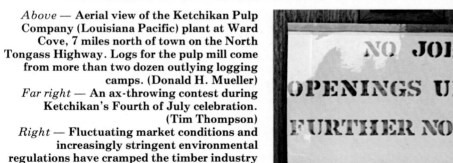

Above — Aerial view of the Ketchikan Pulp Company (Louisiana Pacific) plant at Ward Cove, 7 miles north of town on the North Tongass Highway. Logs for the pulp mill come from more than two dozen outlying logging camps. (Donald H. Mueller)

Far right — An ax-throwing contest during Ketchikan's Fourth of July celebration. (Tim Thompson)

Right — Fluctuating market conditions and increasingly stringent environmental regulations have cramped the timber industry somewhat. This sign was posted at Ketchikan Spruce Mills. (Lael Morgan, Staff)

Left — **Totem Bight park, 10 miles north of Ketchikan on North Tongass Highway, includes several totems and a Tlingit community house. (Doug Wilson)**
Upper left — **Ketchikan's newest major attraction is the Totem Heritage Cultural Center, which includes displays of poles, canoes and artifacts salvaged from former Tlingit and Haida village sites. (Marty Loken, Staff)**
Above — **Totemic faces at Totem Bight park. (Tim Thompson)**

Before the white man, Tlingits relied on the forest to build many essentials of their lifestyle. Canoes and homes of cedar or spruce were hand hewn. Cedar totem poles in front of the houses kept alive the memory of important events or legends. (Large, authentic groups of these sophisticated art forms are found in two parks—Totem Bight, 10 miles north of downtown, and Saxman, 2.3 miles south along the Tongass Highway. The newer Totem Heritage Cultural Center, near downtown on Deermount Avenue, houses ancient poles salvaged from former Tlingit and Haida village sites.)

Ketchikan also remembers another aspect of its heritage—Creek Street, the famous red-light district where Dolly, Black Mary, Blind Polly, Frenchie and others plied their trade for over half a century until 1954. Nearly 20 houses once lined the hillside or were built on pilings over Ketchikan Creek. Not many remain, but some structures have been rebuilt, and new buildings are going up. Besides the totems and Creek Street, points of interest include the one-lane tunnel leading to the west end of town, the town's several small-boat harbors, and the display of ore and minerals, Native and Russian cultures and nautical and fishing history at the Tongass Historical Society Museum. (From the commemorative army fort of Fort Tongass, the view of downtown is spectacular.)

Ketchikan also is known as the Rain Capital of Alaska. An average of 154 inches of precipitation drenches the city every year, and the downpour is measured in feet on a large rain gauge.

Nearly half the visitors touring Alaska are introduced to the state in Ketchikan. Huge passenger ships, often immaculately white, tie at the downtown waterfront or anchor in the Narrows, bringing up to 1,000 visitors each trip during the summer season.

For many the irresistible lure is the king salmon, ranging from 10 to 60 pounds. Many people fish in the annual Ketchikan Salmon Derby, trolling for this elusive fish, which

migrates through the nearby narrow waterways. Some choose to try their luck at Bell Island Hot Springs Resort, Yes Bay Lodge, Waterfall Cannery Resort, or other fishing spots reached by air or private boat. Others seek wilderness cabins provided (for only $5 per night) by the U.S. Forest Service.

Service to the First City is offered by the Alaska state ferry system and through the many daily flights, both north and south, from Ketchikan International Airport. A small ferry owned by the Ketchikan Gateway Borough transports passengers from the airport on Gravina Island to Ketchikan.

Left — A few of the cast members of *Fish Pirate's Daughter,* a local melodrama about Ketchikan's lively early days. (Joe Connolly)
Upper left — The bedroom at Dolly's House was a prime attraction for some during Creek Street's heyday as a red-light district. Dolly's House, minus Dolly and crew, was more recently reopened as a tourist attraction. Last year, following sale to a new owner, the facility was closed to the public. (Lael Morgan, Staff)
Above — Creek Street's boardwalks now lead to refurbished private homes, apartments and shops. (Tim Thompson)

41

KETCHIKAN'S EARLY DAYS

Long before white men reached what is now known as Ketchikan, Tlingit Indians had a summer fishing camp on the banks of a creek where salmon returned in great numbers. The camp was known among the Natives as Kitschk-him or Ketschk's stream; literally translated it means "thundering wings of an eagle."

The first white men in the area were sailors, explorers and traders, who did little more than trade for the abundance of furs trapped by the Natives. Then in the late 1880's salmon attracted the white man to southern Southeastern Alaska. Fish Creek, as Ketchikan Creek was first called, lived up to its name, and in 1886-87 a cannery (which had operated for 3 years at Boca de Quadra) was moved to Ketchikan—white man's pronunciation of the Indian name. It operated as Tongass Packing Company during the seasons of 1887-88 and part of 1889, when it burned and was not rebuilt.

Mike Martin and George Clark built a saltery and trading post around 1890, but the enterprise failed. What revived the town was gold. This glittering metal was found in paying quantities in nearby hills and on Prince of Wales Island. Then copper was discovered, and Ketchikan became an important rendezvous point for miners, prospectors and businessmen.

By the time Ketchikan was incorporated in 1900, it was a booming mining center with a population of 800. Carpenters, saloon keepers, bakers, storekeepers, attorneys and doctors came to this growing town. A transportation company ran boats to the mining camps with supplies and brought the exhausted, fun-seeking miners back to town for occasional rests. Churches, a school, and new business buildings and homes were built. The customs house was moved from Mary Island to Ketchikan, thus making the growing town Alaska's first port of entry.

Mining continued to be a major industry until 1907 when the copper market collapsed. Most of the local mines closed permanently, although a few reopened and operated until the 1920's.

The fishing industry grew in importance at this time, and Ketchikan began its climb toward "salmon capital of the world" status. The first large cannery to be built after the Tongass Packing Company venture and bankruptcy of the saltery, was that of Fidalgo Island Packing Company, which completed its first pack of 10,500 cases in 1900. This was Ketchikan's only cannery until 1912 when three new canneries began operating.

Fresh king salmon was first shipped in 1903, and in 1908 the New England Fish Company Cold Storage bought and froze its first fish. Ketchikan Cold Storage, long a landmark downtown, was built in 1913. The waterfront was soon dominated by fish-processing plants and related support businesses, such as machine shops, ship's chandleries and fishing-supply outlets.

Another dominant feature was Ketchikan Power Company, later called Ketchikan Spruce Mills, built in 1903. In addition to providing lumber for construction of homes and businesses, it cut lumber and timbers for the gigantic cannery buildings. It also produced lumber

HAMILTON, SIMPSON & CO.

MANUFACTURERS AND DEALERS IN

SPRUCE, RED AND YELLOW CEDAR LUMBER,

A SPECIALTY.

PORT GRAVINA SAW MILL.

ORDERS ARE PROMPTLY FILLED.

Port Gravina, Alaska, June 2 1893

Left — **Barkentine sailing ships carried spruce from Ketchikan to Australia in the early 1920's under a contract negotiated by the Ketchikan Power Company, later to become Ketchikan Spruce Mills. (Ketchikan Spruce Mills, reprinted from** *The ALASKA JOURNAL®)*
Top — **An early letterhead of Hamilton, Simpson & Co., an Indian-owned sawmill on the eastern shore of Gravina Island, near Ketchikan. (Patricia Roppel, reprinted from** *The ALASKA JOURNAL®)*
Above — **Air passenger service was inaugurated between Seattle, Ketchikan and Juneau in 1940 by Pan American Airways System, using the Sikorsky flying boat** *Alaska Clipper.* **(Otto C. Shallerer)**

for boxes into which cans of salmon were packed for shipment.

Additional canneries began. Many did not last more than a few years; others changed ownership, sometimes two or three times, but the shiny cans of salmon continued to roll off the lines.

By 1916 six canneries were operating; 10 years later eight canneries in the town of Ketchikan produced half a million cases of salmon. An enormous leap occurred in the next 10-year interval, or by 1936. In that year seven local canneries produced more than 1.5 million cases, and this figure does not include the pack of one of the larger canneries.

As the fishing fleet for both salmon and halibut grew, the need for a protected harbor became apparent. Boats were forced to lay at docks unprotected from wind and waves, and there were no facilities for the mosquito fleet—the nearly 1,000 small fishing boats. A boat harbor, Thomas Basin, was completed in 1933. In 1958 Bar Harbor, at the opposite end of town, provided accommodations for an additional 600 boats and today there are plans to expand it.

As the fishing industry developed and fishing fleet expanded, the need for better navigational aids and for search and rescue became a priority. The U.S. Lighthouse Service built its first facility in Ketchikan in 1912 and moved to its present location south of the city in 1920. During the Second World War the base, by then a part of the U.S. Coast Guard, expanded dramatically and more than 750 men and officers were stationed in Ketchikan. This base became the communications center and supply depot for southern Southeastern and was charged with the responsibility of protecting the waters.

After the war the military personnel resumed maintenance of buoys used throughout the area, servicing lighthouses and maintaining search and rescue operations.

Fishing began to decline and in 1942 nine canneries packed only 350,000 cases. Each year after that the canneries found it harder to make a profit, but fishing continued to be the main support, through the cold storages, until 1954.

That year Ketchikan Pulp Company's $56 million plant at Ward Cove was completed, culminating efforts which had begun in the 1920's to encourage the pulp industry in Southeastern. In 1977 the mill became part of Louisiana Pacific Corporation, as did Ketchikan Spruce Mill, which still operates at the site of its founding in 1903.

Saxman

The Indian village of Saxman (population approaching 300 in 1977) has been growing rapidly in the past several years. A fire hall and many new homes have been constructed, and a small store now offers necessities when there is not enough time for the 5-mile drive to Ketchikan.

Saxman is also the home of the Cape Fox Native Corporation, so named because many ancestors of the Saxman people lived in the Tlingit villages of Tongass and Cape Fox. In the 1890's these people desired schools for their children but were told that only one school would be built. Unable to agree upon which village would have the school, the people set out to find a new home.

Members of the first expedition drowned, and in 1894 a second attempt was made to

Left — Wearing a button-decorated blanket, a Tlingit from the village of Saxman performs a ceremonial dance. Saxman dancers used to perform for visitors, but have given up the practice.
Right and far right — Reproductions of original totems stand at the Saxman totem park, 2.3 miles south of Ketchikan. The original totems came from several area islands — Tongass, Cat, Village and Pennock, and from Cape Fox village. (All by Doug Wilson)

44

select a new settlement. This time a site a few miles south of Ketchikan was chosen. The new community was named Saxman in memory of a teacher who had lost his life in the earlier expedition.

Villagers from Cape Fox and Tongass began the move and soon were joined by the people of Kah-Shakes and by a few from the Tongass tribe in Ketchikan.

A school was immediately built and by 1897 there were 24 houses and a population of 120. A store was opened and at nearby North Saxman, a sawmill, one of the first in the area, cut lumber for the growing towns of Saxman and Ketchikan.

When the people left their original homes, they left their totem poles behind. The U.S. Forest Service launched a program in 1938 to retrieve the poles from Tongass, Cat, Village and Pennock Islands and Cape Fox village.

A park was laid out in Saxman with an approaching driveway bordered by the poles. Reproductions of the original poles, which had begun to deteriorate, were carved. The totems still stand, and the park is a frequent stop on visitor tours.

Metlakatla

William Duncan, a Scottish lay preacher dispatched to northwestern Canada by the Church of England, led about 400 Tsimshians from a settlement near Prince Rupert, British Columbia, to New Metlakatla, Alaska, in 1887. (B.C. Provincial Archives, reprinted from *The ALASKA JOURNAL®*)

Neatly laid out on the west shore of Port Chester on Annette Island is the community of Metlakatla, with a population of just over 1,000. The main economic influences can be seen along the waterfront: a sawmill with log rafts floating in front of the log haul, and bundles of lumber being swung aboard ocean-going vessels generally bound for Japan. Nearby, noisy gulls circle fish-processing plants and the community's fishing fleet. Fishing and lumber have been the economic mainstays of Alaska's first Indian reservation since its beginnings.

The religious migration of a group of Tsimshian Indians led to the founding of Metlakatla. Originally from the village of Fort Simpson, British Columbia, the Tsimshian group moved to Old Metlakatla, B.C., near Prince Rupert, in the mid-1800's. There they lived with their pastor, William Duncan, a Scottish lay preacher sent from London under the auspices of the Church of England. For 20 years the model community thrived, and then Duncan and the authorities of the established church quarreled and Duncan was replaced.

A devoted group of Duncan's followers scouted for a new home and decided on Annette Island in Alaska. Although it was unoccupied at the time of their arrival, it had been, during historic times, the site of a Tlingit village. Legend tells of an attack by Stikine Tlingits, with the survivors moving to Village Island and later Tongass Island.

On August 7, 1887, Father Duncan and 400 Tsimshians dedicated the community of New Metlakatla. Duncan visited Washington, D.C., to lobby for the island, and on March 4, 1891, Congress declared Annette Island a reservation.

The community of Metlakatla was carefully planned and patterned after Duncan's successful colony in British Columbia. Streets were laid out, lots were set aside for occupancy by individual families, comfortable homes were built, a church was constructed, which for many years was the largest in Alaska, a sawmill was established, a salmon cannery was built and put into operation in 1890, and a school was started for the children.

Duncan remained at Metlakatla until his death in

Left — Metlakatla, with a population of just over 1,000, is 15 miles south of Ketchikan on Annette Island. (Jerrold Olson)

Inset — A salmon cannery was established in Metlakatla in 1890. It burned in 1916, was rebuilt 2 years later and has had few interruptions since.

Above — Japanese technicians take a break at Annette Island Packing Company, where salmon roe is prepared for shipment to the Japanese market. The cannery is locally owned, but receives technical assistance from Japanese when packing salmon roe. (Both by Tim Thompson)

1918. During his last few years the operation of the school and salmon cannery were taken over by the federal government. The community continued to prosper, with the tribal council administering the island and community.

The salmon cannery, which burned in 1916, was rebuilt for the 1918 season and leased by the Metlakatla Council through the Department of the Interior for 5-year periods. When the council began to operate the cannery, they retained the name Annette Island Packing Company, and the cannery has operated, except for occasional years, to the present day.

A new cold-storage plant was dedicated in May 1971. Fish are caught by the Metlakatla fishing fleet and by three or four traps in tribal waters. These are the only floating fish traps in Alaska—all others have been outlawed.

To augment the state's depleted salmon runs and help the local fishermen, the community received Bureau of Indian Affairs appropriations for a salmon hatchery on Tamgas Creek. Construction began in the summer of 1977, but it will be several years before the fish return.

During the Second World War a large airfield was constructed and numerous gun emplacements for defense were established on Annette Island. After the war, the base was used by the U.S. Coast Guard for a search and rescue base. Major commercial airlines began to use the airstrip, and small amphibious aircraft—notably the twin-engined Grumman Goose—connected the airfield with Ketchikan, Petersburg and Wrangell.

When Ketchikan International Airport was completed in 1973, commercial use of the airfield on

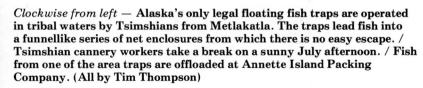

Clockwise from left — Alaska's only legal floating fish traps are operated in tribal waters by Tsimshians from Metlakatla. The traps lead fish into a funnellike series of net enclosures from which there is no easy escape. / Tsimshian cannery workers take a break on a sunny July afternoon. / Fish from one of the area traps are offloaded at Annette Island Packing Company. (All by Tim Thompson)

Annette Island was discontinued. The Coast Guard moved its base from Annette to Sitka in 1977 because the 200-mile fishing limit extended its jurisdiction; Sitka provides a more centralized base for fishery patrols.

With the departure of the U.S. Coast Guard and the commercial airlines, the landing strip is used only occasionally by amphibious aircraft when the water is too rough to land in front of Metlakatla.

Timber has been an essential part of Metlakatla's development. A sawmill has cut lumber much of the time since the original mill was opened by Duncan and his followers. Fire has taken its toll several times, but each time the sawmill has been rebuilt.

Ketchikan Spruce Mills leased the sawmill in 1971 and renamed it Annette Hemlock Mills, because the mill was converted so that hemlock cants could be sawn for export. Louisiana Pacific, Ketchikan Division, operates the sawmill at present.

To serve the community and its visitors, there are two restaurants, an inn, a grocery, gas station, bank and theater. The cottage where Father William Duncan lived has been recently restored and is now an attractive museum. Towering above the community is the Duncan Memorial Church, a replica of the original, which burned in 1948.

Travel to and from Metlakatla is by ferry or by air. Air taxi operators provide charter service to the waterfront in Ketchikan or to Ketchikan International Airport. The state ferry *Chilkat* operates between Ketchikan and Metlakatla on a 2-hour run most days of the week.

49

East of Ketchikan

East and northeast of Ketchikan — "inland," you might say — are misty fjords and hardly settled wild places . . . glaciers of the Coast Mountains, high-country lakes and small, scattered communities.
Below — One of the newer communities is afloat . . . Gildersleeve, a floating camp for loggers working on Hassler Island, north of Ketchikan on Behm Canal, on the northwest side of Revillagigedo Island. (Richard Blakeslee)
Right — A Sitka blacktail doe at Smeaton Bay, which cuts into the mainland 30 miles east of Ketchikan. (Chip Porter)
Far right — The entrance to Walker Cove, part of the Misty Fiords wilderness study area, 40 miles northeast of Ketchikan. Fjords in the area are among the most spectacular in Alaska . . . see following pages. (Stephen Hilson)

Opposite page — A rock wall in Walker Cove shows evidence of glacial carving and scouring. (Mary Henrikson)
Inset photos — New Eddystone Rock, 30 miles northeast of Ketchikan in Behm Canal (Nancy Simmerman), and a waterfall cascading into Walker Cove. (Ken Elverum)
Left — A sheer wall of rock in Punchbowl Cove, 35 miles northeast of Ketchikan in Rudyerd Bay. (Mary Henrikson)

53

Hyder

At the quiet headwaters of Portland Canal, a 70-mile-long salt-water fjord that forms the southern boundary between Alaska and British Columbia, is nestled the once-booming mining town of Hyder, population about 80. A road cut along the steep granite cliffs leads 2½ miles to the adjoining town of Stewart, British Columbia.

Traffic rumbles along this gravel road from Hyder and from the Granduc Mine in Canada. The Granduc Operating Company mines and transports copper ore through one of the world's longest tunnels—53,743 feet (10.2 miles). Since the mine is in Canada, the ore is moved to Stewart where deep-sea loading facilities are available. But today's mining activity is only a shadow of the past.

As far back as 1886 a group of men panned the gravels of the Bear and Salmon rivers and their tributaries in search of placer gold. Although they failed in their quest, they spread the word of the vast potential wealth locked in veins in the mountains.

In the late 1890's the hard-rock prospectors found gold and silver lodes. But there was no real boom, and actual mining work was not attempted until 1901 when the Canadian properties proved workable; Stewart sprung into being.

On the American side, on the homestead of the Lindeborg brothers, the village of Portland City struggled for existence. In 1915 prospectors who retained faith in the American camp applied for a post office. Postal authorities refused to accept the name as there were already too many Portlands in the United States. The group selected the name Hyder for Frederick B. Hyder, a well-known Canadian mining engineer who visited the mines in the Portland Canal area in 1914-15 and predicted a great future for the district.

Hyder's big chance came in 1917-18 when new, rich silver ores were discovered nearby in Canada's upper Salmon River basin. The only practical mode of access to these new properties was through Alaska, and Hyder became the ocean port, supply point and post office for the Salmon River District.

The town began to expand, but there was no place to go. Behind the camp were the steep slopes of the Reverdy Mountains, to the east was Canada, and to the west

Hyder, population about 80, rests somewhat peacefully at the end of Portland Canal, 2½ miles from its only neighbor, Stewart, British Columbia. (Lael Morgan, Staff, reprinted from *ALASKA*® magazine)
Opposite page — Portland Canal, slicing 70 miles into the mainland, forms the southern boundary between British Columbia and Alaska. The head of Portland Canal is one of three places in Southeastern Alaska where overland transportation reaches the sea (a side road from Cassiar Highway 37 emerges at Stewart and Hyder; White Pass & Yukon Route trains cross the mountains from Whitehorse, Yukon Territory, to Skagway — soon to be joined by a new highway — and the Haines Highway meanders north from Haines to join the Alaska Highway at Haines Junction, Yukon Territory). All other towns are connected to the outside world by air or water routes. (Terry Schneider)

Hyder as it appeared in the 1920's when it was a flourishing mining town. Most of the buildings stood on piling over the tide flats because of a lack of flat, dry land. Note the variety of false fronts in this row of wooden business buildings. (Reprinted from *The ALASKA SPORTSMAN*®)

were the swift waters of the Salmon River. So Hyder was built over the tide flats on pilings. Plank streets connected the many buildings. There were at least four hotels, numerous restaurants, bathhouses, pool halls, cigar stores, the Salmon River Banking Company, and a drugstore. There was a doctor, dentist and an attorney. At least two different companies offered to rent pack and saddle horses,

touring cars, trucks, launches and scows. The Loyal Order of Moose and the Hyder Igloo of Pioneers had lodge buildings.

During the boom years, 1920-1930, the population was reported at between 235 and 255 people, but it is more likely that up to 500 people were living in the Hyder area.

Mineralization of the area seemed to pinch out at the border, as mining on the

American side was consistently overshadowed by activities on Canadian soil. Almost all of the production credited to the Hyder side has come from the Riverside Mine. In 1924 a mill was installed and production of gold, silver, copper, lead and zinc continued intermittently until 1950. During the Second World War tungsten also was mined.

More than 50 other prospects in the Hyder area appeared

56

Aerial view of Stewart, British Columbia, 2½ miles from Hyder. Stewart's population is about 1,400 — up and down in the past according to the success of mining ventures in the area. The surrounding mountains and river valleys have yielded quantities of gold, silver, copper, lead and zinc. (Lael Morgan, Staff)

similar to the Riverside but never proved sufficiently rich to mine. Slowly, mining in the whole area was halted and in 1956 the main producer in Canada, the Premier Mine, lost its mill in a fire.

Through neglect, the buildings in Hyder began to fall onto the tide flats as the pilings collapsed, leaving only dry-land structures at the base of the mountains. Today, the sleepy village (sometimes advertised as the "friendliest ghost town in Alaska") has a grocery, curio shop, cafe, motel and three bars—perhaps more bars per capita than any town of its size, at least in Southeastern Alaska.

In 1970 residents of this small community applied for fourth-class city status, the simplest form of municipal government. The request was rejected, and today Hyder remains unincorporated.

The people of Hyder and Stewart have long been served by ships out of Prince Rupert, British Columbia. Most recently, Northland Navigation Company provided barges and ferries, but in October 1976 the towns lost this service when the Canadian government cut off a subsidy to the company. Hyder residents now must rely on floatplanes and a modest passenger vessel for

their connection with Prince Rupert. Other supplies are hauled to town over the long, often rough Cassiar Highway 37, which begins 175 miles southeast at Terrace (or New Hazelton, depending on direction of approach) in British Columbia and winds through magnificent scenery, including spectacular icefalls and glaciers.

The highway has brought quite a few tourists into Hyder, but the few residents survive, for the most part, because of the more reliable traffic between Stewart and the Granduc Mine . . . and their own ingenuity and individualism.

Myers Chuck

A Ketchikan-area harbor favored by the trolling fleet is Myers Chuck (also spelled Meyers Chuck), on the Cleveland Peninsula 40 miles northwest of Ketchikan. Here many a fishing vessel has ridden out a southeast storm which frothed the waters of Clarence Strait into mountainous swells.

Who built the first permanent structure in the cove is debatable. One story tells of an old sailboat captain, Verne Myers, who arrived at the harbor in 1881 with seven men. Together they built a two-story log cabin. Another story says that the village was named for a prospector who found his food in the woods surrounding the harbor.

Food would have been easy to find, and outside the harbor passed countless thousands of salmon each year on their way to the spawning grounds. Records show a Mr. Myers fished a red salmon stream on nearby Union Bay and sold his fish to the Loring cannery in 1898. Perhaps the place was named for him.

First documented activity at Myers Chuck was in 1911, when M. E. Lane started a small hand-pack cannery to utilize the great runs. It is doubtful if the cannery operated for more than a year—in 1914 his enterprise was classified as a mild-cure station where salmon were lightly salted before shipment, and he soon sold the saltery. There is no other mention of permanent fish processing in Myers Chuck.

The largest cannery in the area was at nearby Union Bay, where fish were packed from 1916 to 1945. Floating mild-cure stations came each spring to buy king salmon from the trollers, who continued to visit Myers Chuck when storms blew in Clarence Strait.

A store, public dock and float were available to the fishermen and postal service began in 1922. Cabins were built on land leased from the Forest Service until September 1934, when the townsite was eliminated from the Tongass National Forest.

Population has fluctuated; the estimate in 1938 was 50, but it was far less in later years. Such hearty souls as Fritz the Trap Watchman, Lonesome Pete, Myers Chuck Gus and Halibut Pete kept the winter fires burning. The little village would be dormant except for the radio and weekly mail—the only contact with the world. Life was

58

Opposite page — **A few supplies are available at the fishing village of Myers Chuck — also spelled Meyers Chuck by some residents.**
Left — **Aerial view of Myers Chuck, on Clarence Strait at the southwest end of Cleveland Peninsula, about 40 miles northwest of Ketchikan.**
(Both by Stephen Hilson)

lazy and slow with little to do but eat, sleep and keep up with the firewood. Occasionally cabin-fever feuds would flare—usually ending with the arrival of spring and the fishing season.

Fishing grounds near Union Bay and Myers Chuck eventually were depleted, and then the cannery burned. For a while a fish-buying station purchased the few fish brought in by the die-hards who still made their living trolling for king and coho. A fish buying station was opened by Petersburg Fisheries, Inc. in 1977

so area fishermen no longer must fly their fish to market or make the trip to Wrangell or Ketchikan.

Recently Myers Chuck has begun to grow again (population in 1977 was about 60). Most of the residents are fishermen. The Meyers Trading Post has a store and fuel dock; a public water system supplies water for boats, domestic use and fire fighting, and a portable sawmill has been cutting lumber for new homes.

Because of a communications repeater station behind the

village, there is now a lone telephone, and it is easy to call for a charter airplane to fly out of Myers Chuck. The only other means is by mailboat or private boat.

Inhabitants still live a simple and natural life, spending their summers and long winters in much the same manner as those before them.

PRINCE OF WALES ISLAND

Prince of Wales Island, easily the biggest in Southeastern Alaska, is known for its logging camps, but it also offers places where few have been, and countless small unnamed islets such as the one at left, just offshore in Moira Sound, on the southeast side of Prince of Wales. (Mary Henrikson)

The map at right shows Prince of Wales and some of its larger neighboring islands, as well as principal communities. The gravel road system is expanding steadily as logging operations reach out into new areas.

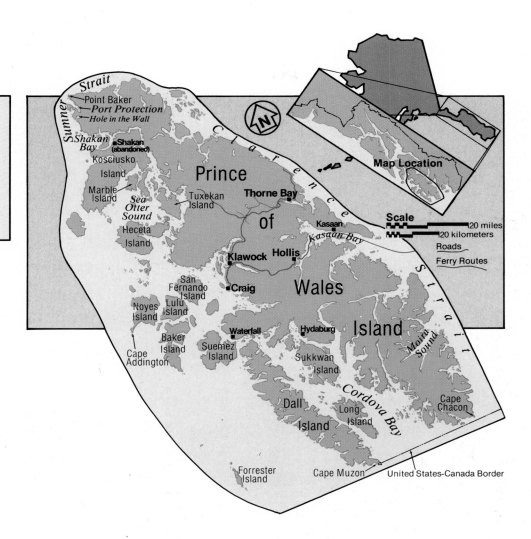

Sumner Strait

Point Baker
Port Protection
Hole in the Wall

Shakan Bay
Shakan (abandoned)

Kosciusko Island

Marble Island

Sea Otter Sound

Heceta Island

Tuxekan Island

Prince

of

Wales

Island

Thorne Bay

Clarence Strait

Kasaan

Kasaan Bay

Klawock Hollis

San Fernando Island

Craig

Lulu Island

Noyes Island

Baker Island

Cape Addington

Suemez Island

Waterfall

Hydaburg

Sukkwan Island

Moira Sound

Cordova Bay

Cape Chacon

Dall Island

Long Island

Forrester Island

Cape Muzon

United States-Canada Border

Map Location

Scale
20 miles
20 kilometers
Roads
Ferry Routes

Four major communities and numerous logging camps and fishing villages are scattered over 2,231-square-mile Prince of Wales Island, third-largest island under the American flag (Kodiak Island is the largest; the big island of Hawaii is second).

Prince of Wales and other members of the island belt on the ocean coast are heavily forested and much of the area has been or is being logged to supply nearby pulp and lumber mills. In 1977 there were 11 logging camps harvesting timber on Prince of Wales and adjacent coastal islands.

Three of the major communities—Craig, Klawock and Thorne Bay—are connected by a gravel road system, which has steadily expanded as a result of logging activities since the early 1950's. The road system continues to grow, offering access to more and more of the island.

The Alaska Marine Highway ferry *Chilkat* began service to Prince of Wales in 1974; now the new ferry *Aurora* makes several trips a week from Ketchikan to Hollis on the east coast of the island.

The Hollis area hosted several gold mines from 1901 to the 1920's; from 1953 to 1962 it was the site of Ketchikan Pulp Company's main logging camp.

Mining has flourished at various

Opposite page — **A quiet shore with waves lapping over rocks in the shallow waters of Moira Sound, on the protected southeast side of Prince of Wales Island. (Mary Henrikson)**
Right— **A petroglyph, carved by early Native inhabitants of Ham Cove, on the southeast side of Dall Island. Design of the rock carving has been highlighted with chalk. (U.S. Forest Service)**
Below — **Hundreds of sea lions gather on rocks near Lowrie Island in the Forrester Island National Wildlife Refuge. Forrester is about 18 miles west into the Pacific Ocean from the outer coast of Prince of Wales Island — a fine spot to live if you are inclined toward the life of a sea lion. (USGS photo by Donald Grybeck)**

63

Above — **A lumbermill at Shakan in the 1870's. The community, now abandoned, was on Kosciusko Island, near the northwest tip of Prince of Wales Island. (University of Washington, Northwest Collection)**

Above — **Men at work in one of the quarries of the Vermont Marble Company on Marble Island, near northwest Prince of Wales Island. The first marble was shipped in 1909, the last in 1932; examples of the product may be seen in the State Capitol Building in Juneau.**

Right — **Coppermount, on Prince of Wales, was the site of two copper smelters built in Southeastern soon after the turn of the century. (W. H. Case photo, Alaska Historical Library)**

times on other parts of this large island and its westward islands. Besides Hollis, gold also has been mined at Dry Pass, Dolomi in Port Johnson, Flagstaff at Karta Bay, as well as at many other prospects. Some silver, lead and zinc prospects were developed but none of the ore was shipped on a big scale.

Copper is the mineral most abundant in the mountains of this island. The region's two copper smelters once operated at Hadley and Coppermount, while at least 15 mines shipped copper ore to smelters in Alaska, Canada and other parts of the United States.

Marble for ornamental use was quarried at Calder, Red Bay, Tokeen on Marble Island, and Dickman Bay in

Fresh from the hold of a fishing
boat, salmon head for the cold storage at
Hydaburg, 22 miles southeast of Craig
on Prince of Wales Island.
(Ken Elverum)

Moira Sound. At View Cove on Dall
Island limestone was quarried and
shipped to Seattle for manufacturing
cement. A uranium mine operates
intermittently at Kendrick Bay.

None of the mining camps have survived, but today all of this area is the
scene of much prospecting activity.

What built the permanent towns was
the salmon. Waters surrounding the
island teemed with these fish, and it
was at Klawock that one of Alaska's
first canneries was built in 1878. In the
following years at least 25 different
canneries were built on Prince of Wales
Island to process salmon.

65

Klawock

The Alaska salmon industry really began here when the first cannery started in 1878. Earlier, in 1868, George Hamilton had combined a trading post with a salmon saltery at this site. He sold his operations to San Francisco-based Sisson, Wallace and Company, who incorporated under the laws of California taking the name North Pacific Packing and Trading Company.

This company built the cannery at Klawock in the same year that a cannery was started at Old Sitka, but the latter did not survive for long. In contrast, the Klawock operations were run by the same company for 51 years without missing a season.

The first cannery buildings, sawmill and store were destroyed by fire on September 18, 1899. By the following spring the company had built a new cannery about a mile south of the old site and on the opposite side of the bay, and it was operational by fishing season.

The sawmill, an essential part of cannery complexes, supplied

Aerial view of Klawock, a fishing village which boasts 21 totem poles and the only airstrip on Prince of Wales Island. (Stephen Hilson)

salmon packing boxes but also sold lumber for local needs. The company also maintained a salmon hatchery from 1897 until 1917 and sockeye salmon fry were released into Klawock Lake. (The old hatchery site is only feet from a large new state-operated hatchery completed in 1978.)

But the North Pacific Packing and Trading Company cannery was not Klawock's only enterprise. A second cannery was started by R. J. Peratrovich in 1920, and Charles W. Demmert opened another one in 1924. Both were run by several companies over the years and both have fallen into ruins.

Today Southeast Seafoods operates the community-owned

cannery, which is a predominant feature of the waterfront.

Another imposing structure is the large sawmill, located across Klawock River on the 7-mile road that connects Klawock with Craig. Obtaining this timber-manufacturing plant was a great boon to the West Coast of Prince of Wales Island. Construction began in 1971 on the Alaska Timber Corporation sawmill, and it shipped its first lumber in July 1973. Since that time it has operated on demand—when orders for its product are received.

Today Klawock is a small town whose 281 residents are primarily Tlingits. The town is built on a hillside facing the water and

Klawock Island. At the top of the hill is one of the largest totem parks in Southeastern Alaska. There are 21 restored original and replica totems from the old village of Tuxekan, a Tlingit winter village to the north where many Klawock people originally lived.

Two lodges have opened to cater to the influx of visitors, many of whom are sportsmen seeking fish and game of the area.

The first airstrip on Prince of Wales Island was completed in 1973 about 2 miles from town. It is the only airstrip on the huge, 130-mile-long island, although there are many floatplane facilities.

A fishing vessel runs into heavy weather near Cape Addington, off the outer coast of Noyes Island. Storms can come up fast in these unprotected waters, sending fishermen scurrying for some of Southeastern's protected bays. (Joe Upton)

George Hamilton, Sr., of Craig, with a traditional halibut hook. A renovated school in Craig was recently named after Hamilton, whose family includes some of Southeastern Alaska's most successful fishermen. (Lael Morgan, Staff, reprinted from *ALASKA*® magazine)

The sawmill and salmon cannery town of Craig was known as Fish Egg in its early years when this photograph was taken about 1912. Later it was named for Craig Millar, longtime Alaska salmon packer who was superintendent of the town's first cannery.

Craig

Craig, with a population of about 500, was once a temporary Indian fishing camp; nearby Fish Egg Island was a favored place for gathering herring eggs during the spring. But it was salmon that led to the founding of the village, and it is salmon that keeps it alive today.

The mild curing, or light salting, of salmon began on Fish Egg Island in April 1907. Craig Millar packed a number of boxes of salmon for Hyman H. Bergman, who represented Lindenberger Bros. Fish Company of Hamburg, Germany.

Operations on Fish Egg Island were so successful that in 1908 Millar constructed a permanent fish station for Bergman on a larger, nearby island. A number of shacks were built by the Natives who came to work. The settlement apparently didn't amount to much because the 1910 census failed to mention its existence.

Mild curing continued until 1911 when Lindenberger Packing Company expanded its operations. A cold-storage facility began freezing fish in the spring, and 20 to 25 buildings were standing by November 1911.

Plans for a salmon cannery, warehouse and store were finalized, and in 1912 the cannery processed its first pack of 57,501 cases. At that time it was the second-largest salmon cannery in Alaska and the third largest of its kind on the Pacific coast.

Prior to the expansion of the Lindenberger interests, the settlement was known as Fish Egg but by 1912 it was officially called Craig, after Craig Millar.

About the time the cannery

Left — **Craig, viewed from the northwest. (Stephen Hilson)**
Lower left — **Waterfall Cannery Resort, southwest of Craig, was launched in 1912 by the founder of Craig. The facility operated as a cannery into the mid-1960's. (Stephen Hilson)**

was in operation, Millar began promoting and building a cannery southwest of Craig at what was to be called Waterfall. After its initial pack in 1912, this cannery expanded numerous times and today the buildings are used as facilities for Waterfall Cannery Resort.

Fish—salmon in particular— continued to provide the livelihood for Craig. Most of the residents were either fishermen, cannery workers or businessmen whose trade was derived from the fishing industry. By 1939 the entire island (reached by a short causeway from Prince of Wales Island) was covered with houses connected by a labyrinth of boardwalks.

In addition to fishing, a sawmill operated in Craig for many years and during both world wars provided high-grade spruce for use in airplane construction. But without wartime contracts, the sawmill ran only now and then, and eventually was closed.

By the mid-1960's Craig was a slowly dying fishing village. Salmon runs were poor and canneries at Steamboat Bay and Waterfall were finally forced to close, leaving Klawock with the only operating cannery on Prince of Wales Island. Craig became a maintenance station for the boats of Columbia-Ward Fisheries, which had purchased the Craig facility in 1959.

A new cold storage opened in 1969, bringing life back to Craig. Built, owned and operated by Lou Scott, it was sold to Craig Fisheries, Inc., in 1971. Today the company continues to operate the cold storage and three fish-buying stations on the West Coast of Prince of Wales—at Kelly Cove, Tokeen and Hole in the Wall.

Craig is centrally located for the West Coast troll fishermen and provides fuel, groceries, restaurants, bars, a hardware store, library, post office and laundromat. The first bank on the island was opened by the First National Bank of Ketchikan in July 1973.

Hydaburg

Hydaburg, with a population of almost 400—mostly Haidas— is 22 miles southeast of Craig . . . accessible only by floatplane or private boat. It was founded in 1911 when the elders of several Haida villages on southern Prince of Wales Island decided to consolidate for better educational opportunities. The villages of Klinkwan, Howkan and Kaigani (first settled by Tlingits, then taken over in the early 1700's by Haidas from the Queen Charlotte Islands) made the move to a site opposite another of the Haida winter homes, Sukkwan.

In December 1911 there were 139 residents in the new village, which was named after the Haidas. E. W. Hawkesworth, the government service teacher, helped the common council to incorporate a trading company to operate a store and sawmill.

Although fishing was the main occupation on the West Coast of Prince of Wales, Hydaburg did not get its first processing plant until 1927. In that year the Far North Fisheries moved its

Sukkwan, one of several Haida villages that merged to form Hydaburg in 1911. This photo was taken around the turn of the century — today the village is abandoned, but one of the totem poles (second from left) presently stands in the lobby of the State Office Building at Juneau. The name Sukkwan is Tlingit, indicating that Tlingits occupied the site before the Haidas moved northward from what is now British Columbia. (Alaska Historical Library)

floating cannery *Pioneer* to Hydaburg, where it was beached and a warehouse was erected on the shore.

The company canned salmon until 1930 when it leased the plant to superintendent Herman Kurth. He called his new business Kurth Fisheries but in 1931 he refloated the *Pioneer* and relinquished the lease.

A permanent, land-based cannery was started in 1935 by Hydaburg Fisheries, Inc., but it lasted only 2 years because runs were light; the building was taken over after a creditor's sale by the Hydaburg Trading Company.

A new cannery was built in 1939 under contract with the Hydaburg Cooperative Association and operated by Hydaburg Canning Company. They canned salmon for 5 years before the Hydaburg Cooperative Association took over the cannery and ran it until 1965. At that time the cannery became a subject of controversy between this association and the Bureau of Indian Affairs, which held the mortgage, and it was closed. Salmon were packed only one year after that—in 1970, when the Shosnoni Corporation of Spokane, Washington, leased the cannery.

McCallum-Legaz Fisheries, a Seattle-based company, leased the buildings in 1971 for a cold storage and in 1974 modernized the plant to a capacity of 1 million pounds. It is operated today by Washington Fish and Oyster Company.

Hydaburg is on a hillside overlooking Sukkwan Narrows; many new homes line the streets and there is a new municipal building. A totem park, laid out artistically above the town, displays restored poles from villages where the townspeople originally lived.

Hydaburg will eventually be connected by road to the main Klawock-Hollis cross-island road, but it is serviced today only by mail plane and charter aircraft.

Left — Totem poles and telephone poles at modern-day Hydaburg. (Vicki Burgess)
Below — Aerial view of Hydaburg, viewed from the northwest. The village, facing Sukkwan Narrows, is the largest Haida settlement in Alaska. (Stephen Hilson)

Upper right — **Logging roads now extend over large portions of central and northern Prince of Wales Island, especially in the Hollis-Craig-Klawock-Thorne Bay area. This photo was taken near Thorne Bay. (Terry Schneider)**
Right — **Leo La Farr, a logger working on northern Prince of Wales Island. (Tim Thompson)**
Far right — **Aerial view of Thorne Bay, Alaska's largest logging camp with a population of about 550. (Lael Morgan, Staff)**

Thorne Bay

While other major communities on Prince of Wales Island are fish-minded, it is the forest that brought Thorne Bay into being. Ketchikan Pulp Company, now Louisiana Pacific, Ketchikan Division, began to harvest timber in the Hollis area in 1953, moving its main logging camp from there to Thorne Bay in 1962.

Located on the shore of Thorne Bay near the mouth of Thorne River, the logging camp is a complete community. There are the customary bunkhouses and mess halls, as well as houses for more than 60 families who make Thorne Bay their home. There is a store, restaurant, movie hall, snack bar, tackle shop and an employee-constructed church. Children can attend school from kindergarden through high school.

A log-sorting and rafting area and a main repair shop are nearby. Today Thorne Bay is considered the largest logging camp in the United States, with a population of about 550.

Until the summer of 1974 all transportation to and from Thorne Bay was by air or water. But now the camp is connected by road to Craig, Klawock and the Hollis ferry terminal.

A troller in the sunset off the coast of Prince of Wales Island. (Tim Thompson)

Kasaan

It was the anticipation of making a fortune in copper that led to the founding of Kasaan. In 1898 a group of New Haven, Connecticut, businessmen purchased a group of copper claims—the most important being the Copper Queen, discovered in 1867 by Charles Vincent Baronovich. This claim has the distinction of probably being the first lode location made in Alaska.

This area was home to a tribe of Haidas who lived at Kasaan (now Old Kasaan) on the north shore of Skowl Arm, on the Southeast Coast of Prince of Wales Island. The Natives began to drift to the mining camp, sawmill and general store at New Kasaan, since shortened to Kasaan. Old Kasaan was the northernmost village occupied by the Haidas in Southeastern Alaska, and was a national monument for a number of years. But fire ravaged the abandoned homes and totems in 1918 and the site lost its status. The totems that escaped destruction have been moved to the Ketchikan Cultural Heritage Center, where they are available for study and display.

Kasaan Bay Mining Company worked the copper claims for several years, then branched out in 1902 to establish a salmon cannery at Kasaan. The company and its enterprises barely lasted 4 years before bankruptcy was declared and the cannery was sold.

The new owners were plagued with bad luck—the cannery burned in 1907, 1910 and again in 1911. Each time the cannery was hastily rebuilt and new equipment was installed in time to pack the season's fish.

Six different companies ran the cannery over the years; the largest pack, made in 1941 by Pacific American Fisheries, totaled 167,451 cases.

In 1938 an experimental pack of razor clams was made. These were brought in the shell from Masset, in British Columbia's Queen Charlotte Islands. For that summer Kasaan was made a port of entry between Canada and Alaska. The enterprise failed, but the cannery continued to pack salmon until 1953.

During the years when the cannery was in production, three stores sold supplies to the fishermen, but there were few other businesses. A school survived for a number of years and was recently reopened. The Presbyterian church, built in 1908, offered services until 1945, but today the building is on the verge of collapse.

Although the Haidas who settled in Kasaan did not construct traditional homes, one had been built on a point of land a short distance from the new village by Chief Sonihat. This became the nucleus for the Kasaan Totem Park, which was built as part of the areawide U.S. Forest Service totem-restoration program started in 1938. Through an agreement with descendants of Chief Sonihat, the Forest Service agreed to restore Whale House, and a number of totems were brought from Old Kasaan to be erected in a clearing among the tall timber.

Under the Alaska Native Claims Settlement Act Kasaan was given full recognition as a Native village, and it incorporated as the Kavilco Corporation. Immediate improvements began as families returned to the village. New homes were built and old ones were remodeled; a new community hall was built and second-class city status was achieved in 1976. Population in 1977 was 38.

There still are no jobs and some of the men have to return periodically to Ketchikan to work for a grubstake. But the future looks good as Kavilco has much valuable timberland and jobs may materialize closer to home.

A U.S. Forest Service crew began salvage work in 1970 on a totem at the site of Old Kasaan, under an agreement with the descendants of Chief Sonihat, who established the village. (Paul Beck)

Point Baker, Port Protection

Separated by a few small islands and a peninsula are the neighboring fishing villages of Point Baker and Port Protection. During the fishing season the two harbors are summer homes to a fleet of boats that fish Sumner Strait and the islands outside Prince of Wales Island. Then, in the fall, the pace slackens and the few hardy year-round residents settle down for the winter months.

Point Baker, on the northwesternmost tip of Prince of Wales Island, was named in 1793 by Captain George Vancouver for the second lieutenant of the *Discovery*, and has undoubtedly provided shelter for fishermen for years. In the late 1930's the Forest Service opened the area for homesites after several fish buyers set up floating stations in the protected harbor. At that time population was listed as 39. (Today's figure is about 80.)

To serve the fishermen who frequented Point Baker, a post office was opened in 1942, and in 1955 the townsite was eliminated from the Tongass National Forest.

Today there are a number of homes along the shores of the

inner harbor. Petersburg Fisheries, Inc. (Icicle Seafoods, Inc.) maintains a fish-buying station, and two stores supply the residents of both Point Baker and Port Protection. When the Point Baker Trading Post and bar burned early in 1974, it was soon rebuilt—the bar is the only licensed liquid-refreshment

establishment on the northern end of the island.

Like Point Baker (and only 2.2 miles south) Port Protection has been used for shelter from the prevailing southeast storms for years. The first recorded use was by Captain Vancouver in 1793 when he found protection for his sailing ships, hence the name.

Upper left — **Aerial view of Port Protection. (Stephen Hilson)**
Above — **Pulling the herring net at Point Baker.**
Left — **A snowy January scene at Port Protection. (Both by Joe Upton)**

A fishing dory and beach-front cabin at Point Baker, at the north tip of Prince of Wales Island. (Joe Upton)

Point Baker, one of Southeastern Alaska's smaller fishing communities, has only about 30 residents during the winter months. (Tim Thompson, reprinted from *ALASKA*® magazine)
Opposite page — The *Kestrel,* a troller skipped by Bruce Gore, emerges from the fog at Port Protection. (Joe Upton, reprinted from *ALASKA*® magazine)

Permanent use of the area began in 1947 at Wooden Wheel Cove, where Laurel "Buckshot" Woolery hauled logs from the nearby forest to build a sturdy store. Buckshot's B.S. Trading Post, had a fish-buying station and a large float with a gangway to the trading post, where he kept a line of groceries, hardware, building and fishing supplies, as well as a museum of artifacts.

A handful of fishermen began to frame small log cabins, woodsheds and outhouses. In 1950 they petitioned the U.S. Forest Service to extend the approved area around Point Baker to include homesites along the north shore of Port Protection. Today a few parcels of land are privately owned, but the majority of the land is leased from the Forest Service.

Buckshot sold his trading post in the early 1970's and his successors managed to keep it open for a year or two. The residents of Port Protection must now travel to Point Baker for their mail and supplies.

But the people who live in these two communities like their isolation. For the past several years—since 1973—a conflict has raged over harvesting timber on the northern part of Prince of Wales Island. Residents have rejected the idea of a road connecting their communities to the rest of the island's fast-growing highway system, and the only means of reaching either site is still by private boat or charter aircraft. Logging activities were diverted to Labouchere Bay, and Port Protection and Point Baker remain havens for the fishermen.

WRANGELL

Coverage in the following section begins with Wrangell, at the north tip of Wrangell Island, and extends north and west to include Petersburg and several islands in Southeastern Alaska's midsection — notably Mitkof, Kupreanof and Kuiu.

Left — A small part of the fleet along the waterfront of Wrangell, which relies heavily on the timber and fishing industries. (Lael Morgan, Staff)

Inset — Aerial view of Wrangell, which had a 1977 population of 3,152. Shakes Island, landlocked in this low-tide view, is at right-center of photo. (Mike Affleck)

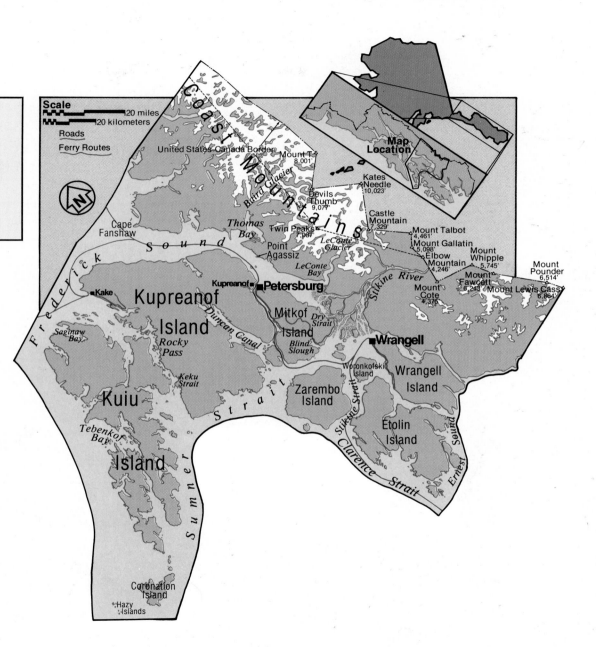

Scale
20 miles
20 kilometers
Roads
Ferry Routes

United States-Canada Border

Coast Mountains

Mount T.
8,001'

Kates
Needle
10,023'

Burg Glacier

Devils
Thumb
9,077'

Castle
Mountain
7,329'

Mount Talbot
4,461'

Mount Gallatin
5,098'

Elbow
Mountain
4,246'

Mount
Whipple
5,745'

Mount
Pounder
6,514'

Thomas
Bay

Twin Peaks
987'

LeConte
Glacier

Mount
Cote
4,375'

Mount
Fawcett
6,213'

Mount Lewis Cass
6,864'

Cape
Fanshaw

Point
Agassiz

LeConte
Bay

Frederick

Sound

Kupreanof

Petersburg

Sitkine River

Kake

Kupreanof
Island

Mitkof
Island

Dry
Strait

Wrangell

Saginaw
Bay

Rocky
Pass

Duncan Canal

Blind
Slough

Woronkofski
Island

Wrangell
Island

Keku
Strait

Zarembo
Island

Sitkine Strait

Kuiu
Island

Sumner

Strait

Etolin
Island

Clarence

Strait

Ernest
Sound

Tebenkof
Bay

Coronation
Island

Hazy
Islands

Map
Location

An older section of the
Wrangell waterfront.
Inset — Three common sights
in Wrangell — floatplanes,
fishing boats and a Japanese
lumber ship loading cants
for a Pacific Ocean crossing.
Wrangell's two mills,
Wrangell Lumber Company and
Alaska Wood Products, are
subsidiaries of Tokyo's
Alaska Pulp Company. (Both
by Tim Thompson)

The busy Wrangell waterfront, near the north tip of Wrangell Island about 85 miles northwest of Ketchikan, features shiny metal cannery buildings, the hum of the lumbermill and patterns of activity on the shipping docks. The nearby boat harbor is a montage of seine boats, pleasure craft, logging tugs and riverboats.

Stretching along Zimovia Strait, the main city (1977 population 3,152) extends several blocks up the slope of a wooded hillside. Many relatively new buildings—most built after the Wrangell fire of 1951 which leveled much of town—line the main street of town, which runs along the waterfront.

Some of Alaska's oldest totemic carvings are found on Chief Shakes Island, reached by a narrow footbridge near the center of the harbor. Here the tribal house of Chief Shakes, a former leader of the Stikine Indians, stands among a colorful collection of Tlingit poles. (The house has been reconstructed three times on this site since the original was built by Chief Shakes. Featuring four ancient and impressive interior houseposts, the building houses tools, carvings and other Tlingit artifacts, all reflecting the culture of the first inhabitants of this area.)

Wrangell's economy is based on commercial fishing and the timber industry. Although the big-time timber

The Chief Shakes tribal house, on a small island near downtown Wrangell, contains four houseposts that are among the oldest in Alaska. (Barry Herem, reprinted from *ALASKA*® magazine)

business is a relative newcomer to Southeastern's economy, Wrangell is the exception. A lumbermill began in 1888. Today, two large lumbermills utilize forest resources provided by 11 logging operations in the area. Both Wrangell Lumber Company and Alaska Wood Products are subsidiaries of Alaska Pulp Company of Tokyo.

Fish and shellfish are the other natural resources upon which Wrangell is dependent. Two canneries process shrimp, crab and salmon, and a cold storage freezes salmon and halibut. Harbor Seafoods, also a subsidiary of

Clockwise from above — **Night view of Wrangell Lumber Company. (Tim Thompson) / Debarked logs are rolled into position to await their meeting with the saw. (Charlotte Casey) / Logs are moved around the sawmill area with mini-tugs. (Tim Thompson)**

Alaska Pulp Company of Tokyo, packs salmon during the season and operates Wrangell's only cold storage. Reliance Shrimp Company processes this tiny delicacy caught in local waters. For a time the company also processed Dungeness crab but landings have dropped sharply in recent years.

Transportation to Wrangell is by water via ferries of the Alaska Marine Highway or by scheduled jet service (inaugurated in 1976). Two cruise-ship lines make Wrangell a regular port of call during the summer tourist season.

For years on the nearby Stikine River shallow-draft boats would wend their way 160 miles to Telegraph Creek, British Columbia. The Stikine, a 400-mile-long river, with headwaters in northern British Columbia, gained fame as an access route to gold fields in the Interior. Commercial boats no longer carry passengers and supplies upriver, so views of the great canyons and glaciers are left to those who own small boats or join river-raft expeditions offered during summer months.

At the mouth of the Stikine River Delta is a garnet ledge that has been exploited since the late 1890's. Today it belongs to the Boy Scouts of America, and youngsters of Wrangell pry the semiprecious stones from the rock to sell locally.

WRANGELL'S EARLY DAYS

Wrangell has lived and grown under three flags and as many different names. It is the only Alaskan city to have existed under the Russian, British and American flags.

The first known visitor was Captain George Vancouver, who surveyed among the islands in 1793. He missed the Stikine River but fur traders who followed soon found it and the Stikine tribe of Tlingits who possessed a wealth of furs.

It was furs of such mammals as the otter, fur seal, mink and lynx which led to the founding of a permanent settlement at the site of Wrangell. In 1834 the Russians erected a stockade, naming it Fort Saint Dionysius, to prevent the powerful Hudson's Bay Company from gathering the fur harvest of the Stikine Valley.

Six years later the Russians leased the mainland of Southeastern to the Hudson's Bay Company, and in 1840 the fort passed into the hands of the British who renamed it Fort Stikine. This became one of a chain of forts that extended from the head of Puget Sound to Fort Durham on Taku Harbor, near present-day Juneau.

The post remained under British rule until around 1850 when it was abandoned. A year after the 1867 purchase of Alaska by the United States, the Americans established a military post, calling it Fort Wrangell in honor of Baron Ferdinand von Wrangell, chief manager of the Russian-American Company from 1830 to 1836. At that time few men lived in the vicinity, and only a few gold miners and

Left — **The Indian village at Wrangell, as illustrated in an 1870 edition of** *Harper's Weekly.*
Below — **The side-wheeler** *Princess Louise* **offloads cargo at Wrangell in 1898, during the Klondike gold rush. The nearby Stikine River was advertised as a shortcut to the gold fields, helping make Wrangell a busy port, and a railroad was projected from Glenora, near the head of navigation on the Stikine, to the Yukon.**

discharged Hudson's Bay men, in addition to the military men and the Stikine Indians, frequented the military post. The post was decommissioned in 1871.

Then came the cry of *Gold!* This precious metal was washed out of the sand bars of the Stikine in 1861, and a few hearty souls braved the elements to pan for gold. But the real boom came in 1872, the year gold was discovered in the Cassiar, in upper British Columbia. One of the easiest routes to the Cassiar was via the Stikine River. Wrangell, at its mouth, started to boom during the winter of 1873, and the military post was reestablished in 1874 to keep law and order.

New buildings rose out of the brush. One of the fort buildings was converted into a dance hall. As gold poured from the Cassiar, Wrangell was merrier than

A Tlingit canoe with two dozen passengers and an American flag near Fort Wrangell in the 1880's. The nameplate reads "Shakes Canoe *Brown Bear*," with a totemic bear carving over the bow. (University of Washington, Northwest Collection)

ever. A metropolis of riotous sport and prosperity developed. Four river steamers plied the Stikine during the open season, hauling the miners' freight to Glenora and Telegraph Creek, near the head of navigation. Then in about 1877, the golden stream ceased. The rollicking, money-spending miners went on to new fields, and the army withdrew from all of Alaska.

Wrangell settled down to a small village on a harbor where the old Indian houses and totems were a dominant feature.

Then, like elsewhere in Southeastern, harvesting salmon became a thriving business. In 1887 Aberdeen Packing Company built a cannery at the mouth of the Stikine, up which hordes of salmon returned to spawn. Two years later the cannery was moved to Point Highfield, about where the north end of the present airport is located. It joined the powerful Alaska Packers Association complex in 1893.

Soon canneries sprang up at nearby Burnett Inlet, Santa Anna and Lake Bay. All used lumber for construction and for wooden boxes for packing the cans of salmon. Wrangell Lumber and Power

Company was built in 1888 to meet these needs.

But gold returned, bringing the next big boom to Wrangell. This time it was the great Klondike gold rush of 1898. Miners again urgently pushed their way up the Stikine River. But the Teslin trail proved to be too far overland to the headwaters of the Yukon. It was easier to use the passes at the head of Lynn Canal. The boom in Wrangell was only momentary—salmon and timber continued to be Wrangell's stable industries.

Alaska Sanitary Packing Company became Wrangell's second cannery in 1912. O. A. Brown, head of the company, was the first man in Alaska to use collapsed and reformed cans, such as those used today. (Prior to this, all cans were made at the cannery from sheet tin.) Then in 1924 the cannery burned and was not rebuilt. Soon after, in 1927, the Alaska Packers Association cannery closed.

During the late 1920's when great runs were making salmon canning a profitable business, three new canneries were built: the Wrangell Packing Company in 1929, the Diamond K Packing Company in 1932

(which had operated a floating cannery at Wrangell since 1927), and ARB Packing Company (the initials of the founder, A. R. Breuger).

After the Second World War these companies began to consolidate their holdings, and in 1947 they became Wrangell Fisheries, Inc. At that time the ARB and Wrangell Packing Company canneries had been inactive for 4 years and the Diamond K cannery had burned in 1946. Binkley's Canning Company packed fish from 1946-1950.

The present cannery, Harbor Seafoods, Inc., was founded in 1949 and has operated most seasons since then.

But salmon canning has not been the only fisheries-oriented business in Wrangell. Wrangell Cold Storage was started in the 1920's and survived for many years. During the 1930's the cold packing of shrimp and crab began in earnest and for a time around 1936, at least three crab and shrimp canneries packed these delicacies. Reliance Shrimp Company is the only survivor. It also was one of the last to hand-pick the shells from shrimp.

In addition to the many cannery operations that started in the 1930's, Wrangell became home to one of two vocational boarding schools for Natives maintained by the federal government. Wrangell Institute was established in 1932, and until 1975 helped bridge the gap between village elementary schools and adult life in Southeastern Native fishing villages. The first residential Young Adult Conservation Corps camp in the United States was opened in the old school in 1978. The goal of this federally funded program is to help find jobs for young people.

The research vessel *SJS*, used in support of salmon-cultivation experiments by the Alaska Aquaculture Foundation, anchored near Etolin Island, south of Wrangell. (Charlotte Casey, reprinted from *ALASKA*® magazine)

PETERSBURG

Left — Alaska's "Little Norway," Petersburg is on the northwest tip of Mitkof Island, roughly midway between Ketchikan and Juneau. As the photo shows, the town faces Wrangell Narrows and Kupreanof Island. At this side of the town is the airport; on the far shore of Wrangell Narrows is the waterfront community of Kupreanof (formerly called West Petersburg), and at the left of the photo is Petersburg Creek, where pink and chum salmon may be observed spawning in late summer and early fall. (Nicholas Wheeler)

Right — Hammers Slough, in the downtown area, is a favorite spot for photographers. (Scott Chambers)

89

S pread over a gentle hillside at the north tip of Mitkof Island, with Wrangell Narrows in front and typical muskeg meadows behind, is the town of Petersburg, population about 2,400. The town basically depends on the gathering and processing of seafood— just as it did when Peter Buschmann founded the community more than 75 years ago.

Hardy Scandinavians, mostly Norwegians, settled Petersburg, and the town has often been described as having a solid and enduring look to it. Since it was never a hastily assembled boom town, streets were neatly laid out, homes were constructed to last and a business district was established along the waterfront.

The main street reflects the economic base: marine and fishing supply stores, banks, hardware and grocery stores, plus the usual businesses that make up a thriving community.

Along one side of the street is the bustling waterfront: fish-processing plants supported by pilings, docks for fuel, barges, ships and ferries, and a large harbor for the fishing fleet.

Petersburg Fisheries, Inc., a division of Icicle Seafoods, Inc., is a large complex of white buildings, on the waterfront. Part of the original 1899-built cannery is still in use in one of the most modern salmon canneries in Alaska.

Clockwise from above — **The night scene in Petersburg. Local residents, many involved in commercial fisheries during the day, unwind at a local bar. / Reflections of the waterfront, viewed from across Wrangell Narrows, with the Coast Mountains in the distance. (Both by Tim Thompson) / Rosemaling, a Scandinavian art form, enhances many Petersburg buildings. An example are the brightly painted shutters on the Sons of Norway Hall, welcoming visitors to the Norwegian "capital" of Alaska. (Dick Estelle)**

The steamy, sometimes eerie world of cannery work shows in this photograph, taken in April as tanner crab were being processed at Petersburg Fisheries, Inc. (Dan Kowalski)

PFI is also the largest diversified plant in Alaska. Salmon, herring, tanner and king crab, and bottom fish, such as pollack, halibut and flounder, are processed. There is also a cold storage, formerly Petersburg Cold Storage, and a plant where fish meal is made for use as an additive in animal feed.

Other processors along the waterfront are the cannery and cold-storage plant of Whitney-Fidalgo Seafoods, Inc., the inactive salmon cannery of Petersburg Processors, and the Alaska Glacier Seafoods operations. At the latter, the famed tiny Petersburg shrimp (plentiful in the surrounding waters) are both canned and frozen.

South of Petersburg at Blind Slough the state operates a salmon hatchery, specializing in rearing coho and king salmon, both of which are favorites of the commercial troll fishermen and the sports fishermen.

Although considered a fishing community, Petersburg has one relatively small sawmill, Mitkof Lumber, outside of town. Eight logging camps and a barite mine at Castle Island use Petersburg as a supply base.

Most of Petersburg's transportation is by water, although Alaska Airlines inaugurated daily jet service in 1976. The town is situated on Wrangell Narrows, one of the principal ship channels of the Inside Passage. Wrangell

Narrows is about 21 miles long, less than 400 yards wide at the narrowest point, and a little more than 1,500 yards wide at the widest point. An extensive system of lights, beacons and buoys mark the passage.

Through this channel come all sorts of floating marine craft—the fishing fleet, tugs with barges, tankers, scows, pleasure craft, cruise ships and ferries. Petersburg is a port of call for the ferries of the Alaska Marine Highway, but not for cruise ships. Thus tourism is not a large factor in the town's economy.

But the town's annual Little Norway Festival each May attracts statewide (and sometimes nationwide) attention. One-day cruises to nearby LeConte Glacier aboard the steel-hulled catamaran *Blue Star* are also a special attraction.

Clockwise from left — **Cordwood? No, stacks of halibut fillets in the deep freeze at Petersburg Fisheries, Inc. / Crab pots await use in Petersburg (both king and tanner crab are processed at PFI). / Tiny, delicious Petersburg shrimp at Alaska Glacier Seafoods. (All by Tim Thompson)**

Left — **An early morning run through Wrangell Narrows to shrimp-fishing grounds aboard the *Charles W,* with her shrimp boom alongside. After a long day of work the crew will return to Alaska Glacier Seafoods, where the little Petersburg shrimp — as they are known — will be canned or frozen. (Tim Thompson)**

93

PETERSBURG'S EARLY DAYS

Although established as a salmon cannery, Petersburg owes its early growth to halibut and much of its continued prosperity to a diversified fisheries. These fisheries began in 1899 under the direction of Peter Buschmann, for whom the town was named.

Buschmann, one of the pioneer cannerymen, set up his first Alaskan operation in 1896 at Boca de Quadra, southeast of Ketchikan. Three years later the company he was connected with planned another cannery. When the site proved unsuitable, Buschmann called attention to a trade and manufacturing site and two homesteads he and his son August had taken up in 1896—the year that August, age 16, built the first cabin at what is now Petersburg.

Here Icy Straits Packing Company began operations in the spring of 1899. A small sawmill, steamer wharf, warehouse, store and bunkhouses were erected.

During construction of the cannery in the winter of 1899-1900, the company engaged in herring and halibut fishing. The Alaska halibut fishery was virtually nonexistent in 1899 and Peter Buschmann, either by accident or design, had picked the perfect halibut shipping point. In nearby Frederick Sound and Chatham Strait were an abundance of halibut. Ice for packing the fish was obtained from floating icebergs and from nearby LeConte Glacier, Alaska's most southerly glacier discharging icebergs into salt water.

The halibut were shipped to Seattle on steamers that regularly plied the Inside Passage. Wrangell Narrows was on the regular course, and steamers diverted no more than a few feet to call at this new port.

The salmon cannery was completed in time to operate during the 1900 season. Over the next 6 years the cannery changed ownership many times and occasionally did not operate at all. Peter Buschmann did not see these years of disorder at the cannery he founded—he had committed suicide in 1903 because of depression over his business affairs.

Even during those years when the cannery was idle, Petersburg continued to thrive. Unlike other cannery sites, where workers and fishermen left at season's end, the people stayed in Petersburg, building a permanent settlement. The halibut fishery proved to be the stabilizer, and Petersburg fathered the first extensive halibut fishery in Alaska.

Gradually more and more fishermen and their families came to settle around the cannery site. Most were Scandinavians who perhaps saw in the Panhandle much that resembled their homeland.

A post office was established January 24, 1900, with Christian H. Buschmann, another of Peter Buschmann's sons, as the first postmaster. By 1905 the population was reported at 100; in 1910 when the town was incorporated, at 585, and in 1977 the population was 2,126.

The community worked together to plan for a progressive future, raising money for a hydroelectric plant, which was opened in 1925—thus providing an excellent source of industrial power for the cold storage, canneries and the town.

A water system was developed.

The Bank of Petersburg, owned and conducted by Petersburg people, was incorporated to promote the financial welfare of the citizens of the town and vicinity. It remained in the hands of Petersburg businessmen until January 1, 1971, when it merged with the National Bank of Alaska.

Fisheries continued to dominate the economy. The cannery packed salmon under control of a local corporation, and then under Pacific American Fisheries. In 1965 Petersburg Fisheries, Inc., was organized by a group of Petersburg fishermen and businessmen and once more the Petersburg cannery was owned and operated by local people.

Over the years a number of other companies attempted to can salmon in Petersburg but most were short-lived. Today the old Kaylor & Dahl Fish Company cannery is operated by Whitney-Fidalgo Seafoods, Inc., which purchased the plant in 1970.

A cold-storage plant streamlined the earlier method of processing fish with glacial ice. Petersburg Cold Storage was begun in the summer of 1926, when 112 residents raised more than $80,000 toward the construction of the plant. For 56 years the cold storage has continued to purchase the Petersburg fleet's fish. In 1972 Petersburg Cold Storage was purchased by Petersburg Fisheries, Inc.

Shrimp have also been important to the economy, and, like the halibut fishery, Alaska's frozen shrimp industry was pioneered in Petersburg. In 1916 Earl N. Ohmer and his brother-in-law Karl I. Sifferman formed the Alaska Glacier Seafoods, a corporation that is still in operation. The two men recognized that the shrimp of Alaska's glacial seas were distinctive in flavor and tenderness. They introduced trawling as a method of catching shrimp and explored the prospective trawling grounds they found within a 40-mile radius of Petersburg.

Several other shrimp-freezing and shrimp-canning establishments have operated in Petersburg over the years, and many of the same processors have also packed crab.

But harvesting the bounty of the sea has not been the only industry. The other natural resource that has contributed to Petersburg's stability is timber. The sawmill built by Peter Buschmann was part of the cannery company's operations until 1917 when it was sold to a group of local businessmen. The original sawmill burned in 1925. Several sawmills have been built and run since then.

Another unique feature in Petersburg for 35 years was the University of Alaska's experimental fur farm, started in 1937 with a territorial government appropriation. At that time there were hundreds of fur farms in Alaska and nearly 60 in the Petersburg area. Studies of various fur-bearing animals such as mink, marten and fox were made, but fur farming in Southeastern waned and in 1972 the last farm was closed.

Nootka lupine (*Lupinus nootkatensis* **), cow parsnips (** *Heracleum lanatum* **), buttercups (** *Ranunculus* **species), and red Indian paintbrush (** *Castilleja miniata* **) brighten a field along the Muddy River, near Point Agassiz, 8 miles northeast of Petersburg. (Jay West)**

Kupreanof

A short skiff ride across Wrangell Narrows from Petersburg is Kupreanof, on the East Coast of Lindenberg Peninsula, Kupreanof Island. Formerly known as West Petersburg, it was incorporated to preserve the independent, rustic lifestyle of its fewer than 50 inhabitants.

The first residents of the present-day site of Kupreanof settled there soon after Petersburg was founded. At one time there was a large mink ranch, but mostly Kupreanof has been a place where rugged individuals could live as they desired.

Currently, as in days of old, each homeowner provides his own water and electrical power. Access is entirely by boat and each resident hauls all goods and materials at his own expense and by his own means. There are no roads or automobiles.

The threat of annexation by the City of Petersburg precipitated the move to incorporate as a second-class city in 1975. Seeing no advantage to

Opposite page — **Kupreanof, across Wrangell Narrows from Petersburg, is a string of beachfront cabins — an independent community whose residents commute to Petersburg by skiff or kayak. (Dan Kowalski)**
Above — **Kupreanof residents share coffee in a cabin that once was the skinning shed on a fur farm — improved considerably with the addition of solid walls, a new used-lumber ceiling, homemade furniture and oil-drum stove. (Marty Loken, Staff)**

becoming part of Petersburg's tax base, the residents chose to form their own government to be able to control the destiny of their area.

The town is adjacent to Petersburg Creek, a proposed wilderness area, and Kupreanof residents not only support the idea but initiated it. They want to

develop their village to be compatible with this wilderness and feel they are now in the best position to do so.

Kupreanof residents enjoy their independent way of life and the natural uncrowded environment the area provides. They intend to perpetuate their way of life.

Left — One of the prime attractions in the Petersburg area is LeConte Bay and
LeConte Glacier, 20 miles east of town across Frederick Sound. (Pete Martin)

Above — The steel-hulled tour boat *Blue Star* works its way through the mass of ice
in front of LeConte Glacier. The boat, based in Petersburg, makes several
glacier trips weekly during the summer. (Tim Thompson)

Kake

Of all the Indians in Southeastern Alaska, the Tlingits from Kake were most dreaded during the 18th and 19th centuries. They frightened Captain George Vancouver during his voyages of discovery in 1793-94, they sometimes terrorized fur traders, and they traveled as far as Puget Sound, leaving a trail of fear behind them.

Then came the famous Kake War of 1869: the Kakes murdered two Sitka traders in revenge for the shooting of a Native by a Sitka sentry. The U.S.S. *Saginaw* was dispatched, and three Kake villages were soon destroyed by fire and shelling.

For years the Kakes did not attempt to rebuild their villages, but finally settled permanently on Kupreanof Island at a site which faces Keku Strait—present-day Kake. In 1891 a government school was established and Aaron Levy built a store. Silas Moon, a Society of Friends missionary and teacher, lived there with his family—and often were the only white people in the village.

The Kakes, along with other Tlingit tribes, traditionally looked to the sea for their livelihood, and in 1912 Kake Packing Company built a cannery nearby. In 1914 it was taken over by Sanborn-Cutting, one of the foremost salmon packing concerns on the Pacific Northwest's Columbia River. They operated the cannery until it was sold in 1926 to Alaska Pacific Salmon Corporation. The cannery changed hands again in 1940 when P. E. Harris acquired it. In the late 1940's the organized village of Kake purchased the cannery, and has operated it since. The 1977 season was a good one and the cannery was leased to Petersburg Fisheries, Inc., giving jobs to many village people.

Logging has also played an important part in the lives of the people of Kake. In the late 1940's timber was harvested from community lands to run a local sawmill. More recently Clear Creek Logging Company became the first logging company in Alaska to use a log-lifting helium balloon. To reduce road building and excessive environmental damage, a huge balloon lifted and moved the logs. The Clear

Overview of Kake, on the northwest coast of Kupreanof Island. (Robert E. Johnson)

Left — **Logging has been important to the Kake area; shown is a log dump on nearby Kuiu Island.** *Below* — **Judy Erickson lends scale to an ancient Tlingit pictograph, painted on a rock wall above Saginaw Bay, west of Kake on the north side of Kuiu Island. (Both by Jay West)**

Creek experiment at Kake ran from 1972 to 1975 as a test of the feasibility of balloon logging.

Kake has been a town in search of firsts and bests. In 1947 the town became the first independent incorporated school district in the territory for all Native children. Then in 1967 the Kake tribe commissioned the Chilkat carvers near Haines to carve the world's tallest totem pole. The village planned this project as part of the state's centennial celebration, and the totem was seen by thousands at Expo '70 in Japan.

After the world's fair, the totem was returned to Kake, and the village held a pole-raising and potlatch, the first such ceremony since the early 1900's. A park is planned to provide an environment in which the Tlingit and Haida cultures can survive and be enjoyed and appreciated.

Today the village, on the northwest coast of Kupreanof Island, is serviced on a daily basis by air taxi businesses from Petersburg, and the *LeConte* stops twice a week. Among the rows of homes and along the waterfront are businesses usual to a small community: a grocery and general store, gasoline station, coffee shop, and hotel. Population in 1977 was 679.

101

SITKA

Continuing north through the
Panhandle, the following section covers
two islands that appear at a glance to be
one — Baranof and Chichagof — and
settlements on both islands including
Sitka, Port Alexander, Tenakee Springs,
Hoonah, Pelican and Elfin Cove.
Left — One of the most familiar views
from Sitka is across Sitka Sound to
3,201-foot Mount Edgecumbe, an
extinct volcano on Kruzof Island, third
largest in the Baranof-Chichagof group.
This photo was taken in early spring.
(Mary Clay Muller)

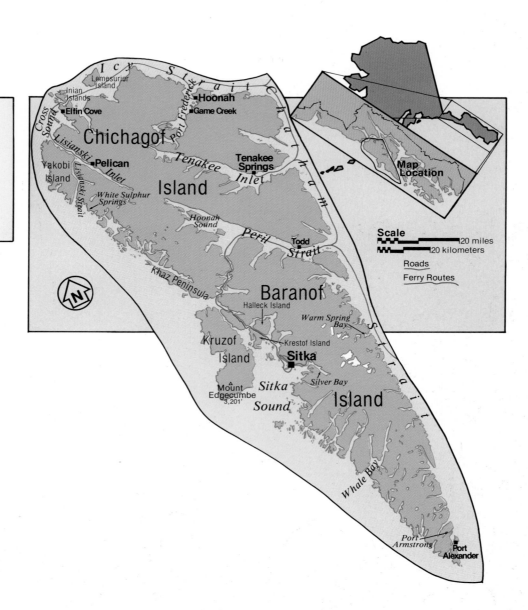

103

Sitka, at the foot of Harbor Mountain on Baranof Island, looks out over an archipelago of tiny islands to the broad sweep of the North Pacific Ocean. Visible a few miles away is snow-capped 3,201-foot Mount Edgecumbe, an extinct volcano often likened to Japan's Mount Fujiyama.

Many of Alaska's historical happenings were recorded at Sitka, and today the town reflects and capitalizes on those historical monuments of its exciting past. Tourism is fast becoming a leading factor in the city's economy. Several cruise ship lines include Sitka as a port of call, and the town, with a population of more than 8,000 will become a favored convention center when two new hotels are in service.

Sitka was the headquarters for the fur-trading monopoly, the Russian-American Company, and the town has retained much of its Russian past. From Castle Hill in downtown Sitka, the sweeping view of the harbor is much the same today as when Alexander Baranof first built his castle there more than 170 years ago.

The Russian Mission, built in 1842 as a boarding school and home for the clergy, is considered one of the oldest original Russian structures in Alaska. Now under ownership of the National Park Service, the building is being restored.

Left — **An old cannon on Castle Hill reminds visitors of Sitka's Russian past. This is where Alaska changed hands on October 18, 1867 — also the site of Alexander Baranof's castle. (Stephen Hilson)**
Above — **The Prospector, a 13½-foot clay and bronze statue, stands in front of the Pioneers' Home. Model for the statue was a genuine pioneer, William "Skagway Bill" Fonda. (Tim Thompson)**

Left — **A sweeping overview of Sitka from atop 2,370-foot Harbor Mountain, north of town. To the left is the eastern channel of Sitka Sound; in the center, reached by bridge from the downtown area, is Japonski Island, host to the Sitka airport. Off on the right horizon is, well . . . absolutely nothing but open ocean. (Nancy Simmerman)**

Left to right — A hang glider settles on the beach of Sitka, with Fuji-like Mount Edgecumbe in the background, 16 miles west of town. (Nancy Simmerman) / A Russian blockhouse replica near the Pioneers' Home. The original separated Russian and Tlingit sections of Sitka when the Tlingits moved back to the area about 20 years after a crucial battle in 1804. (Ed Cooper) / A night view of the O'Connell Bridge, 1,225 feet long, which connects Sitka with Japonski Island. Dedicated in 1972, it is the first cable-stayed, girder-span bridge built in the United States. (Harold Wahlman)

106

Below — **A petroglyph on display at Totem Square in downtown Sitka. Similar rock carvings are found throughout the Northwest and Alaska, roughly from the Columbia River to Cook Inlet, with the heaviest concentration in Southeastern Alaska. They have not been authoritatively "translated," but many feature concentric-circle designs and figures of fish, whales and other creatures. (Nancy Simmerman)**

Right — **Saint Michael's Cathedral, which burned in 1966 and was totally rebuilt, is a focal point of Sitka's history as the capital of Russian America. The original was built in 1844-48, and was considered one of the best examples of rural Russian church architecture. Fortunately, townspeople rushed in to save priceless icons, paintings and religious articles when the fire struck. (Steve Hilson)**

Some of the oldest names in Sitka history are on the crumbling Russian grave markers in Sitka's numerous cemeteries.

In Sitka National Cemetery the oldest burial date is December 1867, 2 months after the purchase of Alaska. Designated a national cemetery in 1924 by President Calvin Coolidge, it was the only such graveyard west of the Rocky Mountains until the Second World War.

But the focal point of Sitka's Russian past is Saint Michael's Cathedral, in the center of town. Built in 1844-48 by Bishop Innocent Veniaminov of the Russian Orthodox Church, it stood for 118 years as one of the finest examples of rural Russian church architecture. Fortunately studies were made and blueprints drawn of this famous structure when it was designated a national historic site, for on January 2, 1966, it burned. Most of the priceless religious articles were saved by the townspeople, and with the blueprints it was possible to construct an exact replica.

Other Russian artifacts are displayed in the Sitka Historical Society Museum (in the Centennial Building), and at the Sheldon Jackson Museum. The latter, on the Sheldon Jackson College campus, contains some of the finest Native arts and crafts and Russian relics found in Alaska—many were collected by Jackson, a Presbyterian missionary,

The New Archangel Russian Dancers offer topnotch Cossack dances twice weekly during summer months. Comprised of local women, the group began their training under a Russian bishop in Sitka. (Tim Thompson)

Below — One of four corner posts for a Haida chief's house on display at Sitka National Historical Park. (Ernest Manewal)
Right — Ellen Lang, superintendent of Sitka National Historical Park, wears a traditional Tlingit ceremonial costume as she tells the story of a new totem being dedicated at the park. (Lael Morgan, Staff)
Far right — Winter view at the park, looking out toward Sitka Sound. (Stephen Hilson)

before he founded the museum in 1888.

Although the Russian past is evident, so is Sitka's Native heritage. Tlingit and Haida cultural items may be seen in the two museums and at Sitka National Historical Park.

At the Visitor's Center Building, Tlingit artisans and students may be observed carving, weaving and learning other crafts. There is also a self-guiding trail leading past several totems to the site of the Tlingit fort, which was destroyed by Baranof in 1804, in the last major stand of the Tlingits against Russian settlement.

The 14 totems and 4 houseposts are exact replicas of the originals which were first exhibited at the St. Louis Exposition in 1904 and the Portland Exposition before being raised at Sitka.

Another landmark is the Pioneers' Home, on the old parade grounds used by the U.S. Army from 1867-1877.

Sitka's past is bringing an increasing number of tourists to the city, bolstering the economy. Major forces in Sitka's economy are the federal government, as represented by the Coast Guard with a facility on Japonski Island, the Bureau of Indian Affairs, the Alaska Native Health

Below — A Native mask on display at Sheldon Jackson Museum, on the Sheldon Jackson College campus, which contains some of the finest examples of Native arts and crafts and Russian relics found in the state. Much of the collection was gathered by missionary Sheldon Jackson. (Stephen Hilson)
Right — A quiet trail through spruce forest at Sitka National Historical Park. (Ed Cooper)
Inset — One of many carvings at Sitka National Historical Park. (Rick Furniss)

112

Left — A colorful Tlingit canoe, carved from cedar, at Sitka National Historical Park. (Rick Furniss)
Below — Two wolf figures are included in this Tlingit housepost totem, carved for a 1904 potlatch in Sitka. The totem is on display at Sitka National Historical Park. (Ernest Manewal)

113

Purse seiners in the Sitka harbor. Fishing dollars today represent a smaller portion of the economic pie in Sitka, but commercial catches of salmon, shrimp, crab and halibut still are processed at Sitka Sound Seafoods. (Tim Thompson)

Service, and the Forest Service, and the Alaska Lumber and Pulp Company at nearby Silver Bay.

At one time fishing heavily dominated the economy, but as the numbers of salmon decreased, canneries closed and then the cold storage burned. Nevertheless, the boat harbor is home to many commercial fishing boats and a large fleet of pleasure cruisers. Commercial catches of shrimp, crab, halibut and salmon are processed at Sitka Sound Seafoods.

Two fish-rehabilitation projects are returning salmon to the area—one operated by the Alaska Department of Fish & Game at Starrigavan Creek, 8 miles out the road from downtown, and another near downtown at Sheldon Jackson College.

Opposite the town is Japonski Island and Sitka's airport, today reached by the O'Connell Bridge—the first cable-stayed, girder-spanned bridge in the United States. Prior to its dedication in 1972 a small ferry connected the island with Sitka. Daily jet service is offered both north and south, and Sitka is a stop for state ferries four times a week northbound, and three times a week southbound. The ferry dock is near the original townsite of Old Sitka, 7 miles north of downtown.

The Alaska Lumber and Pulp Company at Silver Bay, 5 miles east of town on the Sawmill Creek Road. The mill, owned by Japanese interests, was established in 1960 and has been an important factor in the Sitka economy. This view is from Arrowhead Peak, elevation 3,200 feet. (Stephen Hilson)

iron, a sawmill, flour mill and shipyards. Three churches met the religious needs: a Lutheran church; the Church of the Resurrection, set aside for Tlingit worshipers; and Saint Michael's Cathedral.

On October 18, 1867, 2 American generals, 3 navy captains and 250 enlisted men stood in the rain before the governor's house on Castle Hill to take possession of the new American territory, purchased for $7.2 million.

At first Alaska had no governor or government except for its designation as a military district and U.S. customs district. The U.S. Army became the official peacemaker between Natives and the adventurers who arrived after the majority of the Russians left for home. There were a number of wild years before order was established.

In 1884 Sitka became the seat of the first form of Alaskan civilian government, and retained the governmental capital until 1900, when it was transferred to booming Juneau, although the actual move was not accomplished until 1906.

The Presbyterian church was influential in the early days of American Sitka, and its prominent leader, Sheldon Jackson, had his headquarters at what became Sheldon Jackson College. At first a day school was held in the old Russian army barracks, then it was moved to the old Russian-American Company hospital, where it was a boarding school for boys. The building burned in February 1882 and Sheldon Jackson salvaged lumber from the defunct Old Sitka cannery for the first building on the present campus. After that it became a coeducational vocational school, known as Sitka Industrial School, and later expanded to a high school for

SITKA'S EARLY DAYS

Sitka as it appeared soon after Alaska's purchase from Russia. Baranof's Castle is shown in the center of this drawing, flying the American flag. (Alaska Division of Tourism)

Russia's first permanent base in Southeastern Alaska was Old Sitka—then named New Archangel—7½ miles north of present-day Sitka. In 1799 Alexander Baranof built a fortified village as a base for the Russian-American Company's fur trading operations. Three years later in a surprise attack, the Tlingits destroyed the fort, killing most of its occupants. Nothing remains today except a plaque commemorating the site as a national register historic landmark.

Baranof returned with guns and cannons in 1804, defeated the Indians and rebuilt the Russian fort on what is now Sitka.

This early-day settlement became a center of trade and industry for Russian America. Dwellings were built of spruce logs, and a log stockade protected the town. The Indian village stretched along the shore beyond the stockade. High on the hill, near the harbor, stood the governor's house, or Baranof's Castle. Over the years the Russians set up tanneries, a foundry for casting brass, copper and children of all cultures in the territory. The school today is a 2-year junior college open to any student.

In addition to government and education, early-day Sitka was the supply center for Alaska's first hard-rock quartz gold mining operation. The Stewart Mine, 15 miles south of Sitka, was discovered in 1872, and Alaska's first stamp mill pounded the gold from the white quartz. The mine also had the distinction of being the first of many Alaskan gold ventures to flop.

Gold in the immediate vicinity of Sitka did not prove to be in sufficient quantities, but after the turn of the century gold was mined north of Sitka at the Chichagof and Hirst-Chichagof mines.

Salmon proved to be a more stable factor in Sitka's economy. At Old Sitka one of Alaska's first commercial salmon canneries was built in 1878 by the Cutting Canning Company. Unlike the one built at Klawock the same year, Sitka's cannery only operated until 1880, when it was dismantled and moved to Cook Inlet.

For the next 38 years Sitka fishermen sold fish at the Redoubt cannery, a short distance south of Sitka, and later at Red Fish Bay. Booth Fisheries of Chicago built a cold storage in Sitka in 1913, principally for halibut, but in some years also froze salmon. After 1920 there was a good deal of mild-curing of troll-caught salmon in plants in and near Sitka.

Pyramid Packing Company built a salmon cannery in Sitka in 1918 and under a number of different names and ownerships packed salmon through the 1955 season.

Much of the bounty of the sea was frozen at Sitka Cold Storage's plant

which was taken over from Booth Fisheries in 1930. Fish were frozen until 1973 when the plant burned.

It is fitting that Alaska's most historical town would be home for many of the state's pioneers. Before the large three-story Alaska Pioneers' Home was completed in 1935, the home, established in 1913, occupied abandoned buildings of the U.S. Marine Guard and the former residence of the Governor of Alaska. The bronzed clay statue of the prospector, which stands in front of the building, was dedicated in 1949. Sculptured by Alonzo Victor Lewis, the statue was modeled after a real pioneer, William "Skagway Bill" Fonda.

Sitka was a very busy place during the Second World War years. Japonski Island had been a naval reserve since the 1890's, the site of a coaling station and later of a radio communications station, which closed in 1931. After Pearl Harbor the island became a full-scale navy base, and the army built Fort Ray on adjacent

islands. There were gun emplacements on Harbor Mountain and on several other islands in Sitka Sound. The naval station included ammunition dumps and several large seaplane hangars, and there was talk for a time of making it a submarine base.

After the war years, Sitka settled into a quiet existence. It still had Sheldon Jackson High School and Mount Edgecumbe, a Native school and hospital opened at old U.S. Navy buildings on Japonski Island and operated by the Bureau of Indian Affairs. The U.S. Coast Guard continued its operations on a reduced scale, although in 1977 it moved its base from Annette Island and expanded its facilities to enforce the 200-mile limit regulations.

The biggest boost to Sitka's modern-day economy came when Alaska Lumber and Pulp Company built a pulp mill at Silver Bay near Sitka in 1959. Logging camps sprang up in the area to provide the mill with the necessary logs and today 12 camps operate near Sitka.

Top — **Rodman Bay, on the north end of Baranof Island, was the scene of a mining fiasco in the early years of this century. Between 1901 and 1904 Rodman Bay Mining Company spent thousands of dollars to develop a mill and supporting railroad . . . only to discover that there was almost no gold in the lode that was to be mined. (Vincent Soboleff photo, from Alaska Historical Library)**
Above — **An old drawing of Saint Michael's Russian Orthodox Church.**

Port Alexander

Fishing boats at Port Alexander, on the south coast of Baranof Island. (Dorothy Pollard, reprinted from *ALASKA*® magazine)

Up to a thousand fishing boats, mostly trollers, filled the harbor at Port Alexander, 5 miles northeast of Cape Ommaney on the south coast of Baranof Island, during its heyday when the hamlet was one of the main summer centers of the fleet. Today it is a much quieter place, with few reminders that it was once one of the liveliest spots for its size on the Pacific coast.

The trollers began to move to south Baranof Island in 1913 and two floating stations soon joined them to process the salmon. Despite the rather small size of the harbor and narrow, rocky entrance, Port Alexander became the favorite harbor for the fleet that fished Cape Ommaney, Larch Bay and the rest of the outer shore of south Baranof Island.

As additional numbers of boats sold their fish on these grounds, a shore station was started at Port Alexander about 1918 by Pacific Mild Cure Company. Karl Hansen, who became king of Port Alexander's mild-cure operations, began to buy fish at the same time. Over the next 20 years he packed fish and sold supplies to the fishermen. He installed a wireless station and became agent for Standard Oil Company, which installed gas and oil tanks, as well as a water tank to provide the fishermen with free water at the dock.

More and more fishermen came to this lucrative fishing area and buildings went up in the inner harbor. In 1922 there were 200 to 300 boats coming every day to the village, which included 40 houses, 5 stores, 2 bakeries and 4 restaurants. Five establishments dispensed both beer and hard liquor, and across the bay "amusement houses" provided additional recreation.

But when winter came and the storms prevailed, Port Alexander was nearly abandoned. Often only a few watchmen would spend the long, lonely winter repairing and improving the buildings in anticipation of the return of the fleet in the spring.

Because of the narrow rocky entrance and a shallow lagoon within the harbor, many large vessels could not reach the safety of the port. The first improvements were made in 1931 when the port was dredged and some troublesome rock ledges were removed. In 1948 a channel, 40 feet wide and 6 feet deep, was made into the inner harbor, and now most fishing vessels can find shelter from the blasting storms of the North Pacific.

However, as king salmon runs declined, fewer and fewer fishermen returned to Port Alexander, and each year more buildings began to collapse. Finally, in the early 1960's, Richard Gore and his wife bought the remains of Karl Hansen's operations. Today Whitney-Fidalgo Seafoods of Petersburg buys fish in season. A store and fuel dock are about the only businesses remaining in town.

But in a land sale in 1971, 23 lots were sold; new homes have been built and Port Alexander now boasts nearly 50 year-round residents. Like many other small villages in Southeastern Alaska, Port Alexander is being resettled by a steady trickle of newcomers who want to live in a quiet, small community.

A 1959 view of the herring reduction plant at Port Armstrong, 3 miles north of Port Alexander. The plant is now abandoned. (Clay Scudder)

Left — Pink salmon crowd the waters of a stream that empties into Deep Bay, near the west end of Chichagof Island. (Robert E. Johnson)
Above — Todd, population 5, formerly a cannery for which it was named, is now a logging camp on Peril Strait, 9 miles west of its junction with Chatham Strait. (Jerrold Olson)

Right — The rugged west coast of Chichagof Island is a maze of small bays, inlets and islands. The 72-mile-long island was named in 1805 by Captain U.F. Lisianski of the Russian navy for Admiral Vasili Yakov Chichagov. (Robert E. Johnson)

Below — Chichagof Mine, which operated from 1909-1922, was a prominent gold producer. Far right is the original Golden Gate mill. The sandbanks are tailings. The rock dump with snow sheds on top is next to the clubhouse where pool, cards and movies were available to the miners. Residences, a cookhouse, hospital and school cluster are to the left of center. The main mill, where the portal of the mine was situated, is the high building to the left. The two camps on the mountainside in the upper right were accessible from the portal. Bunkhouses and the store warehouse are left of the mill. The mine tender *Ambassador* is at the dock with a barge to haul the concentrate to the Tacoma, Washington, smelter. A gold brick was produced every 2 weeks. The terraced garden of Sing Lee with his store on the beach are in the distance. The mine extended 3,200 feet below daylight in many levels. Operating three shifts per day with 125 men, the mine was closed only on Christmas Day and the Fourth of July. (Courtesy of Laurence Freeburn)

Southeastern has the largest population of bald eagles in the United States (the bird was photographed at Tenakee Inlet on Chichagof Island). The pure white head and neck feathers, characteristic of mature eagles, take about 4 years to develop. (Arthur Bloom)

Tenakee Springs

Man has always sought crevices in the earth where springs gush forth hot mineral water. One such spot in Southeastern is Tenakee Springs, in Tenakee Inlet on the east side of Chichagof Island. Although there are other springs (Goddard below Sitka; Baranof in Warm Spring Bay; White Sulphur Springs on Chichagof; Bailey Bay Hot Springs; and Bell Island Hot Springs near Ketchikan) the most developed is Tenakee Springs.

It was to this spot that many of the early prospectors and miners of Southeastern and particularly of the Interior came to wait out the long, cold winters. About 1895 the springs were enlarged by blasting solid rock to form a large tub. A crude shack was put up so there was a warm, comfortable bathing place. The supply of seafood and game seemed endless in nearby waters and on the mountainsides. What a perfect wintering spot!

In 1899 Ed Snyder, an unsuccessful Klondiker, started

Above — **A sticker on an oil drum expresses the sentiments of some Southeasterners about the future of their state. (Lael Morgan, Staff)**
Upper right — **Tenakee's main street. (Lael Morgan, Staff, reprinted from** *ALASKA®* **magazine)**
Lower right — **Dale Ziel, Al Browne, and Henry Duvernoy in front of one of the new buildings being constructed in the town. The trio came to Tenakee to set up shop as the Ace Boat Building and Exploration Company. (Lael Morgan, Staff)**

Snyder's Mercantile and the store continues to sell provisions to inhabitants of the community.

More and more cabins began to surround the store and the hot springs, and in 1915 the Forest Service constructed a walk and moved various cabins into alignment along it. They also placed a concrete container around the springs to keep out the tide.

Over the years at least three different structures have protected the Tenakee bathers from the weather: a log cabin, possibly built in 1915, was replaced in 1929, and the present concrete structure was built in 1939-40 with matching funds from Tenakee residents and the

124

The buildings of Tenakee cling to the shore of Tenakee Inlet. The town was a popular winter resort at the turn of the century and is now a favorite summer destination. (Jerrold Olson)

Territory of Alaska with Civilian Conservation Corps labor.

The hot springs have been the community's only bathing place—certain hours being specified for its use by men and by women. It has proved to be a relaxing social event.

With the increase of miners, prospectors and fishermen who came to winter at Tenakee, new businesses opened to provide pleasure. There were several institutions, including the Purple Onion and the Shamrock Bar, and gambling was often part of the evening's entertainment. During prohibition these businesses became card rooms and pool halls. Restaurants, the Liberty Theater, a laundry, and a liquor store (after prohibition) were part of the community of Tenakee.

Many of those who came to Tenakee were from what was considered the tougher element

of mining camps, and the town has its Soapy Smith, of Skagway, parallel in Diamond Smith, who was shot in the store by a "good guy." For a time it was necessary to have a U.S. marshal, and the jail frequently hosted visitors.

To add to the activity at Tenakee was a large salmon cannery, 8 miles away near the mouth of Tenakee Inlet. A trail connected the two, and cannery workers frequently spent their days and nights off in town.

The cannery was built in 1916 and operated under various owners until 1927 when it was reorganized as Superior Packing Company. It lasted until 1953, then closed, but in the early 1960's packed crab and shrimp. Today many of the buildings are deteriorating, and the trail is overgrown.

This was not the only seafood processor in Tenakee. Columbia Salmon Company, built in 1918,

closed in 1929 and was finally dismantled in the 1940's. It, like Superior Packing Company, was not in Tenakee, but cannery workers were not discouraged by the 3½-mile walk to town.

When the salmon runs waned and canning became a risky business, crab processing appeared to help bolster the community's economy. Salt Sea Fisheries commenced 10 years of operation in 1938. (The buildings burned in the mid-1960's and all that remains today are charred pilings and rusting machinery.)

The most recent operation was that of Totem Seafoods (1949-1974). The aluminum-clad cannery buildings continue to be a landmark on the Tenakee waterfront—and Tenakee is mostly waterfront. Homes are built side by side on pilings over the water, and only a few perch on the hillside. The main street is a dirt path, and the lone vehicle is

a small truck that delivers fuel oil from a 55-gallon drum.

The largest, most imposing structure is the store with its false front. Other businesses include the Blue Moon Cafe, the Tenakee Tavern, the liquor store, and a small knit and gift shop. The school, which closed after Tenakee's heyday, has recently been reopened.

Today Tenakee, population about 100, is mostly a retirement community, although a few young families have moved in and are building new homes. People from Juneau and Sitka have built cabins in Tenakee, so, unlike the past, the population now booms during the summer months. It has also become a favorite stop for boaters.

The isolated village of Tenakee Springs became a port for the Alaska Marine Highway ferry in 1978—but only for foot passengers.

Hoonah

Hoonah is another of the Tlingit villages which has been occupied since prehistory. Legend tells of an original ancestral home in Glacier Bay, prior to the last glacial advance. Then came the movement of the great ice masses and small bands of people were forced to search for new homes. One group settled a protected site near the mouth of Port Frederick on the north coast of Chichagof Island—a site they named Hoonah, "the place where the north wind doesn't blow."

Long before whites came, the Hoonahs fished along the rocky shores, using shallow lines for salmon and deeper ones for halibut. For a brief time in the late 1700's when fur hunting and trapping were profitable, the men excelled in sea otter and seal hunting. But the fur trade declined and the people returned to a subsistence lifestyle.

The first building erected by a white man at Hoonah was a store of the Northwest Trading Company in 1880. In the following years the Presbyterian

Above — Wind and rain have weathered many of Hoonah's early buildings. Recent efforts, however, have led to new housing construction and installation of sewer, water and power facilities.
Upper right — Hoonah, population about 1,000, depends on fishing and fish processing for its livelihood.
Lower right — Third and fourth graders pay close attention to Glenda Daugherty at the Hoonah school.
(All by Tim Thompson)

126

Hoonah, on Port Frederick, has a sheltered harbor for seining and trolling fleets. (Michael Nigro)

This cannery, first built in 1908, continues to pack fish when salmon runs in the northern part of the Panhandle warrant it. In 1977 Excursion Inlet and the cannery at Kake were the only ones to operate north of Petersburg.

A disastrous fire in 1944 burned many homes in the heart of Hoonah, and also destroyed traditional ceremonial costumes and keepsakes that had been handed down for generations. Even with governmental help, the job of rebuilding was hard. But in recent years Hoonah has made great strides toward becoming a modern city—housing shortages have been remedied, and new sewer, water and power systems have been installed. The village's population, 748 in 1970, is now about 1,000.

Crab processing in Hoonah has continued, and Hoonah Seafoods is a prominent part of the waterfront. Thompson's Cold

Home Mission opened a church and school. An 1887 report describes the town as consisting of 19 houses, including the mission and trading store, with 450 to 500 people wintering in the village.

Being close to Icy Strait, Hoonah fishermen shared in the swarms of salmon which passed by on their way to inland streams. Fishermen sold fish to canneries at Dundas Bay, Bartlett Cove or Excursion Inlet. Then in

1912 Hoonah Packing Company built a cannery about a mile north of town, and 4 years later enlarged it.

Other seafoods were packed over the years by various companies. Canned hard-shelled clams were experimented with around 1932; a mild-cure floating processor also was active in the 1930's; Alaska Glacier Seafoods Company of Petersburg canned crab at Hoonah in 1936; and in the mid-1930's one of Alaska's

first king crab canneries was in operation on a floating barge at Hoonah.

Icy Straits Salmon Company was incorporated in 1934 to take over the salmon cannery which had been closed since 1923. The company packed salmon until 1953. With the closure of the Hoonah cannery, most of the seine fleet and many of the cannery workers spent their summers at the Excursion Inlet cannery directly across Icy Strait.

127

Above — **Filleting salmon is a cooperative effort at the Game Creek agricultural community.**
Right — **Children are a big part of the life at Game Creek, a 5-mile skiff ride from Hoonah. (Both by Tim Thompson)**

Storage processes much of the fishing fleet's harvest.

A Juneau air taxi provides service to the community, which offers a gravel runway in addition to the traditional floatplane ramp. The Alaska Marine Highway vessel *LeConte* serves Hoonah three times a week. Although vehicles can be brought to Hoonah, the road system in and around town is extremely limited.

In recent years a new 72-acre agricultural settlement, Game Creek, has sprung up 5 miles west of Hoonah, founded as a Christian community by a group of determined pioneers—most from the East Coast of the Lower 48. Game Creek (technically known as the Mount Bether Bible Center) had 115 residents in late 1977 who were continuing to plant healthy vegetable crops, build cabins and work toward becoming a self-sustaining community.

Transportation from Hoonah to Game Creek is by boat.

Left — A community portrait at Game Creek, which was settled in 1975. (Tim Thompson, reprinted from *ALASKA®* magazine)

Lower left — John Lepore shows off a turnip, one of a variety of vegetables grown at the agricultural settlement.

Below — Work horses were among the first possessions brought to the 72-acre plot which the settlers call "The Land." Here one of the animals pulls lumber for new construction. (Both by Tim Thompson)

Pelican

Built mainly over the water on stilts with a boardwalk down the center is the Chichagof Island fishing village of Pelican. Lining the walks are a store, a few cafes, steam bath, small library and Rosie's Bar, where hundreds of names are carved in the bartop. But it is the cold storage that is the life line to this village of some 140 people.

And it was this cold storage that started the settlement in a small cove, on the rocky shores of Lisianski Inlet. The story of the founding of Pelican is the story of Kalle Raatikainen, and it is said he built the town because he was tired.

Kalle was a fish buyer and during the early 1930's he bought salmon on the west coast of Chichagof Island, from Khaz Bay north to Deer Harbor on Yakobi Island. Scows were anchored in harbors near the fishing grounds to receive fish, but to transport these to Sitka Kalle used his diesel-powered boat, *Pelican.*

Because it took so long to reach the processors in Sitka, he vowed that he would build a cold-storage plant closer to the fishing grounds, and it would be a town built by fishermen and for fishermen.

Finding a site was no easy job, but find one he did—one of the few white fishing villages in Southeastern whose site was so intentionally selected. It had a protected harbor for fishing boats, but deep enough for ocean

Clockwise from below — **A protected harbor for fishing boats, but deep enough for ocean steamers were main points Kalle Raatikainen considered when he established Pelican on the east shore of Lisianski Inlet. / Lisianski Inlet cuts 25 miles into the northwest coast of Chichagof Island. (Both by Stephen Hilson) / Rosie's Bar, a relaxing spot for the hardy residents of Pelican. (Lael Morgan, Staff)**

steamers to come in for the frozen pack. A sizeable stream tumbled down the mountainside in a series of falls and cascades, thus furnishing both fresh water and power. The only thing it was short of was flat space, but there was enough for the cold storage and a small town.

Kalle drove his claim stakes on August 2, 1938, and since his fish packer *Pelican* was a stout and faithful vessel, he decided Pelican would be a good name for his dream town.

Next a corporation, Pelican Cold Storage, was organized and when the fishing season ended the two fish-buying scows were towed to the new site. One was beached and converted to a cookhouse and mess hall. The other was anchored and became a bunkhouse and warehouse. The first building erected on land was a Finnish sauna, with a store and office connected to it.

Fishermen and others drifted in to start work. Lumber, heavy timbers, creosoted pilings, building hardware and machines for a sawmill arrived. Once the sawmill was set up, construction lumber zipped off the saw blades.

An application for a post office was made, and in November 1939 Pelican's post office was opened with Robert De Armond as the first postmaster. Soon there were enough children for a school.

But funds were slow in coming for the cold storage. In 1941, Laurence Freeburn leased the Pelican Cold Storage for $900 from the Alaska Transportation Company, which had acquired the property. Freeburn brought in Pros Ganty as a partner and established a cannery in the present fish house, producing 18,000 cases under the name of the Cape Cross Canning Company.

A cannery was built in 1942 and a joint operation was conducted with A. R. Brueger (of the ARB Packing Company in Wrangell) on a floating cannery tied to the dock in 1943. The new cannery was operated in 1944, but a bad season forced sale of Cape Cross to the Whiz Fish Company, which in turn sold out in 1949.

Products of the sea have continued to arrive in Pelican for freezing and other processing. The town was incorporated as a city, and increasing numbers of people spend the winter here, even when the fishing is closed.

Above — **The summer fishing fleet anchored at Pelican.**
(Robert E. Johnson)
Left — **Art Bloom, in a kayak, brings in a load of Dolly Varden near Pelican.**
(Bruce H. Baker)

131

Elfin Cove

Above — Elfin Cove, with year-round population of about 35, is near the north tip of Chichagof Island, 15 miles south of Glacier Bay National Monument. (Marty Loken, Staff)
Right — The local post office. One of the more notorious residents of Elfin Cove is Harvey, the chicken who lives at the post office. (Stephen Hilson)

Another of the several troller villages in Southeastern Alaska is Elfin Cove, tucked in a sheltered bay near the north tip of Chichagof Island. It is a seasonal place that bulges with boats of every size and shape during fishing season from April to September, and then is quiet, often lonely, during the long winter.

The first name given this cove was "Gunkhole," the fishermen's name for any protected spot with a narrow opening to the sea. Near the largest salmon fishing banks in Southeastern, the Fairweather Grounds, Elfin Cove is a natural place for fishermen to gather. It has a fine harbor with a safe anchorage. Although its entrance is only 45 feet wide, the bay opens like a flask.

The first recorded operations in the cove began in 1927 when a fish buyer named Hutchinson arrived with two boats, the *Resolute* and the *Comet*, to mild-cure salmon. Unfortunately, the *Comet* capsized early in the season and all barrels and

132

supplies were lost. Hutchinson gave up in disgust.

So Ernie Swanson, who bought fish and had a fox farm on Three Hill Island, decided to move in, renaming the Gunkhole Elfin Cove after his boat, the *Elfin*. As time went on he moved from a floating operation to shore, where he built a store, restaurant and dock. As fish buyer and merchant he presided over the Swanson Store until his death in 1971. Others have tried to run the store but it now stands empty.

A second fish buyer arrived in the 1940's. John Lowell built another dock, warehouse and store. He soon added a restaurant for trollers, who after a week at sea appreciated a meal cooked by someone else.

In the early days when fishing was closed on Sundays, hundreds of trollers and purse seiners came to the cove to take on supplies and water (which was piped down the mountain), so they would be ready to fish on Monday. Now fishermen come in at the end of a trip to unload fish and get ice. They also come in on days when the great Pacific Ocean is too stormy to venture forth.

At Elfin Cove everything is connected by boardwalks and most structures are built over the water on pilings. Juneau Cold Storage has a fish-buying barge with a modest store during the summer, but there is no store during the winter and people must go to Pelican or Juneau for groceries.

JUNEAU

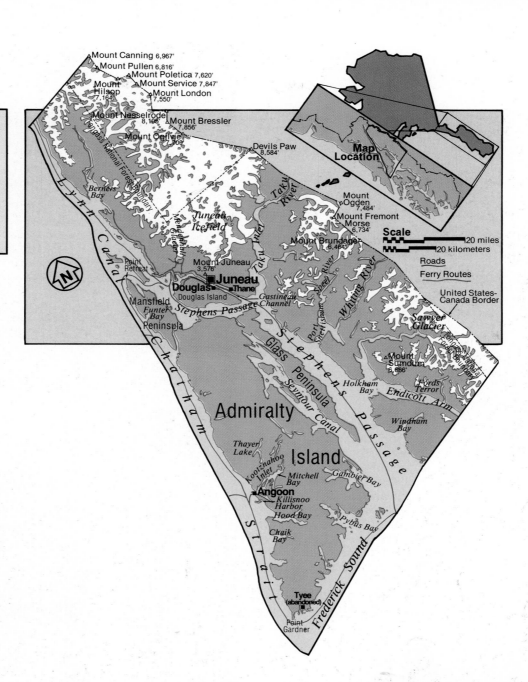

Mount Canning 6,967'
Mount Pullen 6,816'
Mount Poletica 7,620'
Mount Service 7,847'
Mount
Hilsop
7,164'
Mount London
7,550'
Mount Nesselrode
8,105'
Mount Bressler
7,856'
Mount Ogilvie
709'
Devils Paw
8,584'
Map
Location
Mount
Ogden
7,484'
Mount Fremont
Morse
6,734'
Tongass National Forest Boundary
Juneau
Icefield
Taku River
Mount Brundage
6,464'
Scale
20 miles
20 kilometers
Roads
Ferry Routes
United States-
Canada Border
Lynn Canal
Berners
Bay
Mendenhall Glacier
Mount Juneau
3,576'
Point
Retreat
Juneau
Douglas
Thane
Taku Inlet
Sheep River
Whiting River
Sawyer
Glacier
Mansfield
Peninsula
Funter
Bay
Douglas Island
Gastineau Channel
Stephens Passage
Port Snettisham
Port Houghton
Mount
Sundum
6,666'
Fords
Terror
Glass Peninsula
Stephens Passage
Holkham
Bay
Endicott Arm
Seymour Canal
Windham
Bay
Admiralty
Thayer
Lake
Island
Gambier Bay
Kootznahoo Inlet
Mitchell
Bay
Angoon
Killisnoo
Harbor
Hood Bay
Pybus Bay
Chaik
Bay
Chatham Strait
Tyee
(abandoned)
Point
Gardner
Frederick Sound

This section, as indicated by the map, includes North America's largest city (in terms of square miles, Juneau leads all with 3,108); sparsely populated Admiralty Island, and a series of dramatic fjords indenting the mainland southeast of Juneau — Taku Inlet, Port Snettisham, Holkham Bay, Tracy Arm, Endicott Arm, Fords Terror and Windham Bay. Juneau is third-largest city in Alaska in terms of population (1977 figure for the area was 20,465), and Admiralty Island is distinguished by North America's greatest concentration of bald eagles, and a healthy population of Alaska brown bears.

Left — Dramatic overview of Juneau and Gastineau Channel from a ridge on Douglas Island. Directly behind the downtown area is Mount Juneau (3,576 feet), and farther off in the distance is a small slice of the Juneau Icefield. At right of downtown, on the sidehill above Gastineau Channel, stands remains of the Alaska-Juneau (A-J) Mine, shut down in 1944; to the right of the mine and extending into the channel is a large flatland created with fill material from the mine. (Wayne Jensen)

Nestled against a towering backdrop of Mount Roberts (3,819 feet) and Mount Juneau (3,576 feet) is the state's capital, Juneau. The modernized skyline stands out against these cliffs, its government office buildings, hotels and stores confined between the mountains and Gastineau Channel. The winding streets are narrow and hilly — many one way — with steep wooden stairways leading to homes on the hillside.

Dominant in downtown Juneau are numerous government buildings, reinforcing the fact that in the capital city more than every other job is government-related. Chief among these are the Federal Building, the newer State Office Building, perched on the hillside, the State Court Building and the brick and marble-columned Capitol Building. Juneau also is home for Sealaska, the Southeastern Alaska regional Native corporation, which has built a large white office building in downtown Juneau.

The residential community of Douglas — actually part of Juneau — lies across Gastineau Channel and is connected by bridge. The suburbs also have expanded into Mendenhall Valley on land leveled by the still-receding Mendenhall Glacier.

A shopping center next to the airport provides most of the needs for these

suburbanites. In addition to the Juneau business district there are commercial areas in Douglas and Auke Bay.

Considerable evidence of the old days makes Juneau a favorite stop for visitors, many of whom arrive on cruise ships. Among popular sites is the Alaska State Museum, which includes a wide-ranging display of Eskimo and Indian artifacts, and extensive collections of the geological, animal, bird and plant life of this vast and varied state.

Other attractions are the House of Wickersham, where memorabilia of Alaska's Judge James Wickersham, one of the early judges and politicians, are displayed. Not far away, hemmed in and almost hidden by new buildings, stands Saint Nicholas Russian Orthodox church, with its cross, mosquelike dome and colorful circular architecture. Built in 1894, it has been in continuous use since that time. The stately Governor's Mansion looks more like a

137

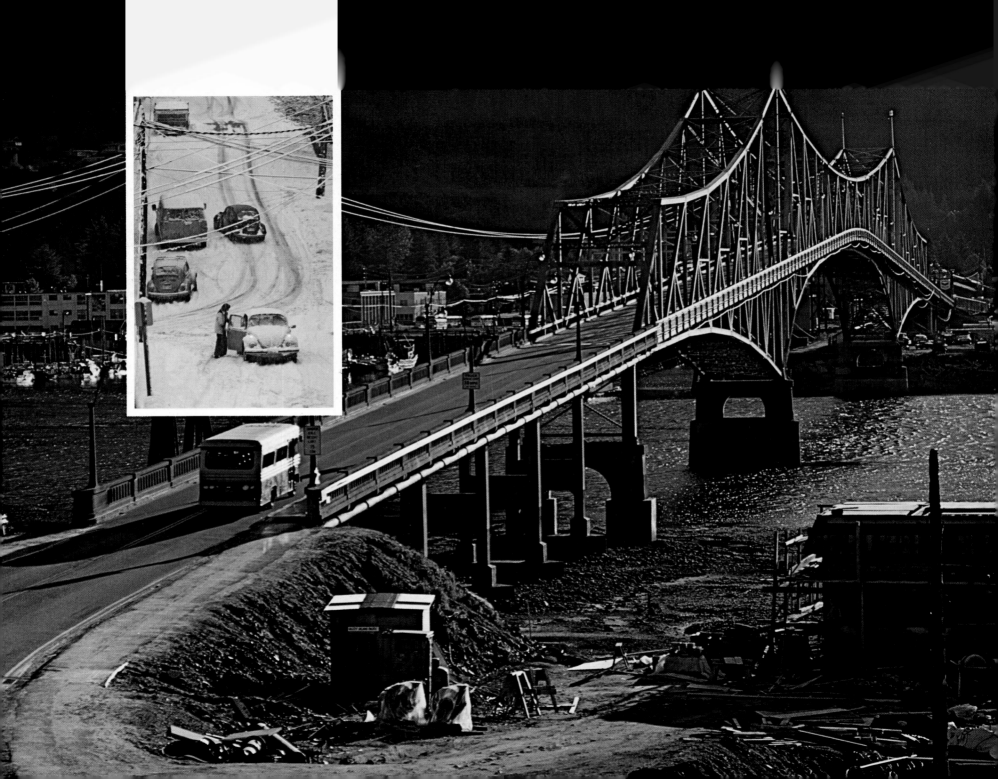

southern plantation house than the home of Alaska's governor.

Remains of the gold era are few. A new museum has been opened at the Last Chance Mine, part of the Alaska-Juneau (A-J) Mine. The trail to Silver Bow Basin follows Gold Creek, which once was harnessed to provide water for the mills and placer operations and ends at the site of the Perserverance Mine, where only footings remain.

At Thane, south of Juneau, nothing remains of the old Alaska Gastineau Company operations except a few building shells along the trail to the rusting remains in the forest.

Modern highways provide access to the scenic trails, campgrounds and beaches. They also lead 13 miles north to Mendenhall Glacier, the only glacier accessible by road in Southeastern. Here there is a visitor information and observation center.

Winter sports enthusiasts enjoy abundant powder snow at Eaglecrest, on Douglas Island, Southeastern's only developed ski resort. The Juneau area also has extensive trail systems which offer cross-country skiers many miles of scenic exploration.

Immediately to the east of Juneau, over the first ridge of mountains, is the Juneau Icefield, a 40- by 100-mile spectacular expanse that is the source of all glaciers in the area, including Mendenhall, Taku, Eagle and Herbert. (The

best way to see the ice field is via charter flightseeing on a clear or high-overcast day. Flights usually take 30 to 60 minutes.)

Southeast of Juneau are several dramatic inlets and fjords — Taku Inlet, Port Snettisham, Holkham Bay, Endicott Arm, Fords Terror and Windham Bay — reached by charter boats or aircraft.

Sports fishing is another big attraction. The Golden North Salmon Derby, a 3-day event in August, draws many fishermen who vie for prizes. King salmon fishing is often so good fishermen forget to tell of the coho salmon and halibut which strike their

Above — **The State Capitol Building, with marble columns from a now-abandoned mine on Marble Island, northwest of Ketchikan. The legislature meets here every January . . . and February, and March, and April . . . (Lael Morgan, Staff)**
Upper right — **Busy downtown Juneau. (Tim Thompson)**

lines. Anglers are happy with the abundance of fresh-water fish and hunters find no shortage of birds and animals. Charter boats and several lodges in the area — including Glacier Bay Lodge at Bartlett Cove, near Gustavus, and Thayer Lake Lodge on Admiralty Island — provide excellent accommodations for outdoorspeople who seek more remote corners of Southeastern.

Left — **Connecting Juneau and Douglas (really part of Juneau) is a narrow, aging bridge — sometimes considered for replacement but still serviceable. (Marty Loken, Staff)**
Inset photo — **Steep hillsides and other features have led to the description of Juneau as a "little San Francisco" . . . not so charming when the hills become ski runs. Shown here is Harris Street in January. (Mark Smith)**

Clockwise from above —
Mendenhall Glacier and Lake, viewed from near the U.S. Forest Service visitor center, 13 miles north of Juneau. (John Helle) / Flying just above the crevasses of Mendenhall Glacier, a small aircraft — near center of photo — looks even smaller. (Mike Affleck, reprinted from *ALASKA*® **magazine) / An ice cave near the snout of Mendenhall Glacier. (Tim Thompson) / Late winter view from a waterfront house at Auke Bay, north of Juneau. (Jerrold Olson)**

140

Left and below — Researchers have been studying the Juneau Icefield for years, checking snow depths, monitoring weather, tracking glacier movements and accomplishing other scientific tasks — sometimes under conditions far worse than illustrated here. (Both by Ross Miller)

Left — Devils Paw, an 8,854-foot peak along the Alaska-British Columbia border, is 36 miles northeast of Juneau — part of the huge Juneau Icefield. (Stone Flower Studio)

Opposite page — The race is on as boats scramble for fishing grounds at the start of the Golden North Salmon Derby, an annual 3-day event held in August. (Jerrold Olson)

Left — A summertime view of Eaglecrest ski area, on Douglas Island, which features a day lodge, chair lift and two ski tows. (G. R. Tromble)

Below — Auke Bay, 12 miles north of Juneau, includes one of five small-boat harbors in the Juneau area. (Jerrold Olson)

145

JUNEAU'S EARLY DAYS

The early days in Juneau were exciting but surprisingly orderly considering that gold led to its founding.

A pair of hired gold seekers, Joseph Juneau and Richard Harris, working for a Sitka mining engineer, prospected along the mainland shore northward from Cape Fanshaw. Near the mouth of a creek they named Gold Creek, the pair found placer gold but failed to follow the stream. Sent back to the site by their employer, Juneau and Harris landed on some of the richest gold-bearing ground ever discovered in what became known as the Juneau Gold Belt.

They staked the first claims there on October 4, 1880, and on the 13th anniversary of the transfer of Alaska from Russia, Juneau and Harris staked a townsite, which they called Harrisburg.

News of gold on Gastineau Channel got around with amazing speed and dozens of men headed for the new strike. With

A historic flag-raising. At noon on July 4, 1959, the 49-star American flag was hoisted to the top of one of the two flagpoles in front of the Memorial Library at Juneau, marking the final step in Alaska's admission to the Union. The Alaska state flag — eight gold stars in the form of the Big Dipper and Polaris on a field of blue — went up on the other pole. The balloon, carrying another 49-star flag, was set aloft soon after the picture was taken. (Robert N. De Armond)

Alaska under jurisdiction of the Navy Department, several officers and a detachment of Marines were sent to the new camp to keep order, perhaps making it the only gold strike in history supervised in its early stages by the U.S. Navy.

Harris soon fell into disfavor so the camp was renamed Rockwell, in honor of a lieutenant commander who headed the new naval post.

As soon as the snows melted in the spring of 1881 the miners made for Gold Creek Valley. By the end of the year 281 men had recorded mining or town-lot claims, or both. And, near the end of the year, the camp once more changed its name—this time to Juneau, in honor of the other discoverer of the rich strike.

A post office was established early in 1881 and with it came regular monthly steamer service, bringing more gold seekers as well as merchants and tradesmen.

Development work progressed rapidly at the mines. Miles of ditches and flumes were constructed to carry water to the sluices. Hydraulic nozzles replaced picks and shovels on the placer grounds.

Within 10 years of the discovery, a wagon road ran from town to Silver Bow Basin at the head of the valley. W. I. Webster built the first stamp mill in 1882, and it was followed by nearly half a dozen others working on ore from the many lodes.

The earliest major development, however, was across the channel on Douglas Island, where in the spring of 1881 Pierre Joseph Erussard discovered a lode claim, which he sold to John Treadwell. This became the famous Treadwell Mine, where a reduction mill was built in 1882.

At the peak, Treadwell mills dropped 880 stamps and employed hundreds of men in the mills and mines. The town of Douglas developed to provide services for these mines.

Juneau, meanwhile, was growing rapidly. Its first decade saw the start of schools, churches, a hospital, two weekly newspapers, a couple of breweries, hotels, saloons, restaurants, a cigar factory and mercantile and service establishments of all types.

From the earliest days, Juneauites took an active part in the political affairs of Alaska, and Alaska's first political convention was held there in the summer of 1881. Juneau more than ever became a trading and transportation center, and in 1900 incorporated as a first-class city. The capital was officially transferred from Sitka to Juneau in 1906.

Fishing and lumbering were added to mining as primary industries. A sawmill was built and at least seven salmon canneries operated at various times in the immediate Juneau-Douglas vicinity. The halibut fishery, aided by the availability of glacier ice for shipping fish to market, also became a sizable business. (Ice came from Taku Glacier or from the great bergs that used to drift into Gastineau Channel.)

Races between huge dugout canoes, carved from spruce or cedar logs and manned by Alaska Natives, were features of Fourth of July celebrations at most Southeastern Alaska towns in the early years of the century. This race took place at Juneau in 1907. Each canoe had 14 paddlers. (Alaska Historical Library)

Mining, however, was still the major industry. At Thane, 4 miles south of Juneau, the Alaska-Gastineau Mining Company built a huge mill to work ores which were carried 2 miles through a mountain tunnel from Perseverance Mine in Gold Creek Valley.

Other mines at Funter Bay, Berners Bay, Yankee Cove, Eagle River, Snettisham, and Windham used Juneau as a supply base.

Closer to Juneau, the Alaska-Juneau Mining Company built a mill and mine which in time became the world's largest gold mine, in terms of tonnage handled daily. This company furnished jobs for up to 1,000 men. The enormous quantities of waste rock provided fill materials for acres of waterfront land and was used to build a breakwater to protect Juneau's harbor.

But mining suffered a heavy blow on April 22, 1917, when part of the Tread-well mine caved in. Although the rest of the mining operations were run on a small scale for a few years, the population of Douglas (for a time larger than Juneau) began to diminish. Then fires struck in 1926 and 1937, but a cross-channel bridge provided road connections and Douglas survived as a suburb of the larger community.

Juneau began to assume an air of permanence as modern concrete buildings replaced the wooden structures of the gold camp days. The Territorial Legislature gained a home in 1931—the Federal and Territorial Building, which is now the state Capitol Building.

The mining era came to an abrupt halt at midnight, April 8, 1944, when the Alaska-Juneau Mine was closed by governmental order as a wartime manpower conservation measure. The impact on the local economy was not nearly as great as might be expected. The mine had been operating on a reduced scale, and the town was enjoying a wartime boom.

By the end of the war, both federal and territorial agencies expanded and in 1959, when Alaska was proclaimed a state, Juneau became its capital. But in 1974, Alaskan voters chose to move their capital to the northern part of the state. In November 1976 voters selected a site near Willow, 65 road miles north of Anchorage, but funds to build the new city have not yet been fully appropriated. The move, if it takes place, should be in the early 1980's.

With the closing of Juneau's last lumbermill and the continued fishing decline, Juneau has been looking for diversification of its economic base to make up for the impact of moving the government.

Lode gold mining began at Treadwell on Douglas Island in 1884 with an open pit and a five-stamp mill. The pit can be seen at left center of this picture and became known as the Glory Hole. Eventually the operation expanded to four mines whose ore was crushed in five mills dropping 880 stamps, with nearly 2,000 employees in all. Three of the mines were flooded by a cave-in on April 22, 1917, and forced to close. The fourth mine ceased operations in 1922. By then the complex had produced nearly $67 million in gold bullion. (W. H. Case photo, Alaska Historical Library)

East and southeast of Juneau, along the mainland side of Stephens Passage, a series
of bays and fjords indent the coastline — carved mostly by glaciers descending from
the Coast Mountains.
Left — An old cabin along the shore of Holkham Bay, 45 miles southeast of Juneau.
Above — West Twin Glacier dumps into a lake near the head of Taku Inlet,
25 miles east of Juneau. The glacier originates 5 miles inland in the Juneau Icefield.
(Both by Pete Martin)

Opposite page — Icebergs slowly drift
out of Endicott Arm, a 30-mile-long fjord that
extends northwest from the terminus of Dawes
Glacier to Holkham Bay, 44 miles southeast of
Juneau. (Pete Martin)

Left — Rock cliffs rise 3,000 to 4,000 feet above the
cold waters of Fords Terror, a dramatic estuary that
dumps ice into Endicott Arm. The fjord is so named
because of its narrow entrance area, where churning
tides and icebergs create a dangerous situation for
boaters. (Stephen Hilson)

Above — A classic round-sided glacial valley,
carved over centuries near the head of Tracy Arm.
This view is to the north, with Tracy Arm barely
visible in the distance. (USGS photo by Donald Grybeck)

151

Admiralty Island

Above — Layers and layers of mountains near the north end of 96-mile-long Admiralty Island, south of Juneau. (Stone Flower Studio)

Right — Stan Price, one of Admiralty Island's best-known bush residents, tends his garden at Pack Creek, near Windfall Harbor on the west side of Seymour Canal. (Richard Bayne)

Opposite page — The sometimes-floating home of Stan Price. (Soapy Lingle, reprinted from *ALASKA*® magazine)

Opposite page — Calm waters along the east side of Admiralty Island, with Glass Peninsula and islands of Seymour Canal in the foreground. (Pete Martin)

Left — An Admiralty Island brown bear relaxes with dinner along Pack Creek, on the east side of the island. Many of Admiralty's bears fall into the *Shiras* color phase — an almost black "brownie" unique to the island. (John Crawford)

Angoon

The ancient Tlingit village of Angoon is the only permanent community on Admiralty Island. The Native village corporation, Kootznoowoo, wants to keep it that way, and federal legislation was recently introduced in an effort to make Admiralty Island a wilderness preserve.

The island was home to the Hutsnuwu tribe of Tlingits long before the arrival of the Russians at Sitka. Industrial development began near the town in 1880 on a small island, Kenasnow. Here Northwest Trading Company started a trading post and whaling station known as Killisnoo. The Angoon Natives were engaged to hunt the whales.

On one of the hunting trips a premature explosion of the charge in a whaling harpoon killed a shaman who was a member of the crew. When restitution of a number of blankets for the death was demanded, the superintendent sought aid from the U.S. Navy. The naval ship *Adams* conducted the operation but was too large to go inside the harbor, so in 1882 the revenue cutter U.S.S. *Corwin* bombed and burned Angoon, although no one was injured or killed because the village had

been evacuated. It was not until 1973 that the final resolution of this event was made. At that time the U.S. government paid $90,000 to the village as restitution for the bombing.

Whaling did not last at Killisnoo, and the company switched to herring processing, but went bankrupt in 1885. A new company, Alaska Oil and Guano Company, took over the business, and it thrived for 45 years until the plant was closed in 1930.

During the early years new methods of fishing for herring were introduced and with the increased catch, there was a need for additional help. More and more of the Angoon Natives moved to Killisnoo, where they worked in the herring-processing plant, educated their children at the U.S. Bureau of Education

Left — The revenue cutter U.S.S. *Corwin* burned and bombed Angoon in 1882 following an incident involving the death of a Tlingit shaman aboard a whaling boat. The controversy that followed was not resolved until 1973 when $90,000 was awarded the City of Angoon for damages. (University of Washington, Northwest Collection)

Below — A humpback whale surfaces in Kootznahoo Inlet with a mouthful of herring. Whales were hunted from a station at nearby Killisnoo in the early 1880's by the Northwest Trading Company, which hired Angoon Natives to pursue the whales. For many years after the whaling effort, herring were reduced for meal and fertilizer and salted for food sale. (Robert A. Henning, Staff)

Left — Aerial view of Angoon, Admiralty Island's only permanent settlement. (Stephen Hilson) *Inset photo* — Angoon's waterfront, sometime around the turn of the century.

The salmon purse seiner *Jerilyn*, Captain Peter Jack, of Angoon, at work in Chatham Strait on the west side of Admiralty Island. Crewmen aboard the boat are hauling in the purse; lines to the left go to the smaller seine skiff, which is helping hold the *Jerilyn* away from the net during the retrieval process. (Joe Upton)

school, and began to worship in the Russian Orthodox church.

Then on June 8, 1928, fire swept through the village, destroying about 39 buildings, including the school, church and post office. Many of the people moved back to Angoon rather than rebuild.

Today, as in the past, Angoon is basically dependent upon the natural environment. Subsistence hunting and fishing, berry picking and root gathering are a way of life. Intense commercial fishing has largely depleted the once-plentiful salmon and halibut runs.

Although the village has never had a cannery, many of the Angoon Natives fished for the Hood Bay cannery, originally built in 1918 by Hidden Inlet Canning Company. This cannery, its traps and floating property were sold to the Angoon Community Association in 1948, but runs were so small in the area that the cannery could not be profitably run. It fell into disrepair and eventually was destroyed by fire.

Many of the people still fish but for the last few years commercial seining in the area has been closed or limited to one

Bunkhouses at an abandoned cannery at Hood Bay, south of Angoon on the west side of Admiralty Island. (Joe Upton)

or two days. With so little money to spend on improvements, the villagers have relied heavily on state and federal programs to alleviate critical housing conditions. Under these programs housing has doubled since 1973. The Alaska Native Brotherhood has built a large hall, and a new state-operated school provides education. A fire truck, purchased with Betty Crocker coupons, protects the village.

Angoon is a dry community, without bars, but there are two motels, one with restaurant facilities, and two general stores.

Movies are shown several nights a week in two or three private-home commercial ventures. Until a few years ago the village had no telephones.

Access to Angoon has been limited in the past. Mail came three times a week by air, and charter flights were frequent. For decades residents relied on barges to transport supplies. All of this changed in the summer of 1977 when service to Angoon was begun by the Alaska Marine Highway ferry *LeConte*, which brings in foot passengers, automobiles, and van loads of freight twice a week.

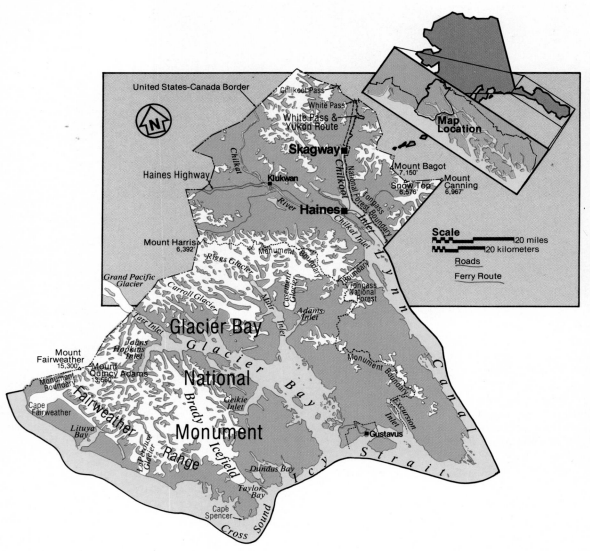

United States-Canada Border

Chilkoot Pass

White Pass

White Pass & Yukon Route

Skagway

Haines Highway

Klukwan

Chilkat

Chilkoot Inlet

Chilkat Inlet

River

Haines

National Forest Boundary

Tongass National Forest

Mount Bagot 7,150'

Snow Top 6,576'

Mount Canning 6,967'

Mount Harris 6,392'

Monument Boundary

Riggs Glacier

Grand Pacific Glacier

Carroll Glacier

Muir Inlet

Casement Glacier

Adams Inlet

Tongass National Forest

Boundary

Lynn Canal

Glacier Bay

Tarr Inlet

Johns Hopkins Inlet

Glacier Bay

National

Monument

Monument Boundary

Mount Fairweather 15,300'

Mount Quincy Adams 13,560'

Monument Boundary

Cape Fairweather

Fairweather Range

Brady Icefield

Geikie Inlet

Excursion Inlet

Lituya Bay

La Perouse Glacier

Dundas Bay

Gustavus

Taylor Bay

Cape Spencer

Icy Strait

Cross Sound

Map Location

Scale

20 miles

20 kilometers

Roads

Ferry Route

GLACIER BAY & VICINITY

The following section is dominated — at least in terms of square miles — by Glacier Bay National Monument, one of Alaska's major wilderness attractions. Also included are towns and villages in the Glacier Bay-Lynn Canal region . . . Gustavus, Haines, Klukwan and Skagway.

Glacier Bay National Monument, 50 air miles west of Juneau, includes 16 active tidewater glaciers; icebergs from these glaciers dot the waters of Glacier Bay and its many inlets. Access to the monument, for most visitors, is via nearby Gustavus and the Park Service headquarters at Bartlett Cove. Some visitors, however, go on flightseeing trips over the monument from airports at Juneau, Haines or Skagway.

Glacier Bay Lodge, facing Bartlett Cove in Glacier Bay National Monument, houses many visitors to the area. Tour boats make daily trips into Glacier Bay and its inlets. (William Boehm)

Gustavus

Gustavus, on the north shore of Icy Passage at the mouth of the Salmon River and 48 miles northwest of Juneau, has been described as a happy Sleepy Hollow sort of place that would remain unchanged if those who live there had their way.

Settled in 1914 by three newlywed couples who homesteaded, Gustavus has been an agricultural center—as much as anything else—since then. The fine, broad fields and acres of flat grasslands enticed the early settlers to select this level area for their homesteads.

Many of the oldtimers made their living from cattle, because the herds could graze for themselves most of the time. Beef, berries and garden stuffs were marketed, for the most part, at nearby canneries.

Today's year-round residents live in homes well spaced apart on plots carved from the original homesteads. When summer comes, additional residents arrive in the tiny community (1977 population about 91) to enjoy the quiet, homey atmosphere.

The community lacks TV, stores, movies and other conveniences, but nobody seems to mind. There is a post office, a small school and an airfield, which was built in the early 1940's.

Visitors en route to Glacier Bay deplane here and are bussed to Gustavus Inn or Glacier Bay Lodge (at Bartlett Cove). Gustavus Inn, famous for its hospitality, was once a farmhouse and still has the feeling of a homestead. Its owners maintain beautiful flower and vegetable gardens and raise chickens, geese, sheep and ponies.

Gustavus has no natural boat harbor. During construction of the airport, Morrison-Knudsen Company dug out a harbor in the Salmon River for its barges. This has sufficed as a boat harbor, but small craft must wait for high tides before negotiating the river. Mailboats and larger ships use a dock, which extends into Icy Strait for what seems an interminable length.

In the 1940's much of the area was included in Glacier Bay National Monument and is no longer open for homesteading. A few newcomers are settling here, buying subdivided pieces of the old homesteads, and many parcels of land have been sold to out-of-state residents.

Opposite page — **Harbor seals in Muir Inlet, Glacier Bay.**
Left — **Mountain goats often are spotted by passengers aboard tour boats in Glacier Bay, especially in Muir Inlet. (Both by Michael Nigro)**
Below — **The** *Fairsea* **in front of Margerie Glacier, near the head of Tarr Inlet — a big ship that looks quite small by comparison. (David Nemeth)**
Bottom — **The tour boat** *Thunder Bay* **passes through a mass of icebergs near McBride Glacier. (Tom Bean)**

163

Far left — Ice-filled Muir Inlet, photographed at sunrise. Glacier Bay was called "big ice-mountain bay" by Tlingits, and was described in 1879 by John Muir as "a picture of icy wildness unspeakably pure and sublime." The monument, part of the Fairweather Range of the Saint Elias Mountains, covers 4,981 square miles, making this reserve the largest in the National Park system. While many visitors come to Glacier Bay and see the principal inlets and glaciers, relatively few explore the monument's huge back country and outer coast. (Michael Nigro)

Left — A multicolored field of flowers near the Dundas River, which flows into Dundas Bay on the south side of Glacier Bay National Monument. (William Boehm)

165

Above — The face of La Perouse Glacier, which heads on the south slope of Mount Crillon in the Saint Elias Mountains and flows 15 miles to the Gulf of Alaska, at the midpoint along Glacier Bay National Monument's outer coast.
Right — Sunset along the outer coast of the monument, with the face of La Perouse Glacier at right. The glacier was named for a French navigator who mapped the coast area in 1786. (Both by William Boehm)

Lynn Canal

East of Glacier Bay National Monument and north of Juneau is Lynn Canal, a 60-mile-long passage that was first explored in 1794 by Captain George Vancouver. Between the Chilkat Range and the Coast Mountains, Lynn Canal is an unpredictable stretch of water lacking waterfront communities — except at its north and south extremes.

Below — A Piper Super Cub on the shore of Lynn Canal, midway between Juneau and Haines. (Rick Furniss)

Right — A midwinter gale blows in Lynn Canal, dropping the temperature — including consideration of the chill factor — far below zero. (Mary Henrikson)

At its north end, Lynn Canal splits into two main channels, Chilkat Inlet (to the left), and Chilkoot Inlet (to the right). In the center of photo is 11-mile-long Chilkat Peninsula; Haines is barely visible at the far end of the peninsula, and Skagway is 16 miles farther north near the end of Taiya Inlet. Muddy water at right is dumping into Lynn Canal from Katzehin River. (William Boehm)

Haines

Surrounded by mountains and facing Lynn Canal, the continent's longest and deepest fjord, Haines (1977 population 1,366) offers scenery, sports fishing and a blend of Native culture and pioneer history. From the narrow peninsula near the head of Chilkoot Inlet where Haines is situated, Davidson Glacier sparkles in the sun, and to the north can be seen the peaks of the White, Chilkoot and Chilkat passes— all routes to the Klondike.

When the Russians first came to the Chilkat Valley it was populated by Indians living in several large villages. These people owned and jealously controlled trails from the coast into the Interior.

For centuries the Chilkat Indians had trekked over the Chilkoot Pass, a steep, icy trail, with heavy packs of dried salmon and fish oil, which they bartered for furs in the Interior.

White people were at first barred from crossing the mountains, but eventually the Chilkats launched a lucrative business of transporting men and their goods over the rugged passes.

With the white people came their religion. S. Hall Young, a Presbyterian missionary, visited the area in 1879 with his friend John Muir, the naturalist. After this visit plans were made for a Christian town with a mission and school. By 1881 a site was chosen on

Haines (foreground) and Port Chilkoot, with Portage Cove on the left and Chilkat Inlet on the right. (Pete Martin)

the narrow portage between the Chilkat River and Lynn Canal.

It took a number of years for old-timers to stop calling the place Chilkoot and consider another suggested name, Willard Mission. Neither name stuck, and a post office was established in 1884 using the name Haines, in honor of the secretary of the Presbyterian National Committee of Home Missions, which raised funds for the new mission.

When the fur-trading days were over, Haines began to grow as a gold mining supply center. Prospectors outfitted or picked up last-minute supplies before heading over the Dalton Trail, an alternative route to the Klondike.

Then gold was discovered in the Porcupine District, about 36 miles upriver from Haines. From 1899 until the mid-1920's many thousands of dollars' worth of placer gold was washed from the gravels of the Porcupine River and its tributaries.

Like other Southeastern towns on the water, fishing has played an important part in Haines' history. Lynn Canal, Chilkoot and Chilkat inlets abound with salmon. Even today, with declined fish runs, each summer and fall finds a large gill-net fleet setting drift nets in the often rough waters.

Although the Chilkat and Chilkoot region is no longer a fish-processing center, it was once the scene of much salmon-canning activity. In 1882, just 4 years after salmon canning began in Southeastern, M. J. Kinney built Chilkat Packing Company, and a year later in Pyramid Harbor, across Chilkat Inlet from Haines, Northwest Trading Company also started a cannery. Neither lasted for long: Chilkat Packing Company burned in 1892, and

171

the Pyramid Harbor cannery, after burning and being rebuilt, was abandoned in 1908.

Other short-lived cannery operations were at the Chilkat Indian village (1889-1893), Chilkoot Packing Company at the head of Chilkoot Inlet (1900-1904), and Alaska Fisheries Union in Chilkat Inlet (1902-1908). Haines Packing Company, which was incorporated in 1917 by local people, canned salmon intermittently at its Letnikof Cove location until 1972.

Today Haines lacks operating canneries and cold storages. Haines Packing Company continues to buy fish during the season but packs the fish at the Excursion Inlet cannery, near the south end of Lynn Canal.

Another influence on Haines was the military base at Chilkoot. In the early 1900's the U.S. government requested the release of 100 acres of land at Port Chilkoot for a permanent military base, the first such post in Alaska. Fort William H. Seward was established in 1904, named for the Secretary of State who negotiated the purchase of Alaska. But in 1923 the name was changed to Chilkoot Barracks.

Abandoned in 1943, the post was purchased by a group of veterans who used the former officers' residences for their homes and proceeded to repair, renovate and redecorate the old barracks as a tourist resort. Today the

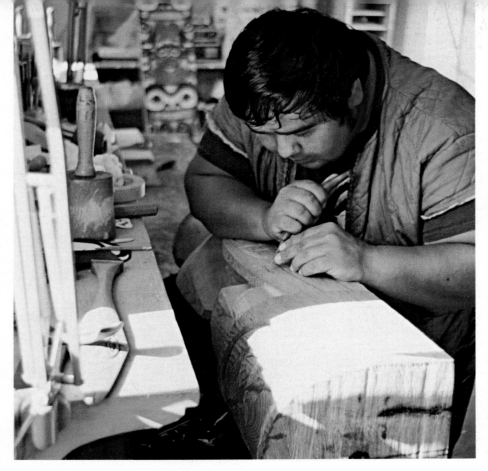

Cliff Thomas, a Tlingit carver, works on a small totem pole at Port Chilkoot. (Jack VanHoesen)

grounds include Totem Village, with its striking totems and Raven Tribal House, where revived Chilkat crafts of carving and weaving are practiced. The artists and Chilkat Dancers are sponsored by Alaska Indian Arts, a nonprofit organization devoted to the revival of Tlingit art and culture.

Port Chilkoot and Haines merged as one community in March 1970. The community relies heavily on tourism, and there are exceptionally good visitor facilities—with the added plus that

Haines enjoys a drier, sunnier climate than other parts of the Panhandle.

The annual Southeast Alaska State Fair is held each August at the fair grounds, and people from all over Southeastern cheer the horse races, delight in the entertainment and contests, and examine the many entries in the fair.

Much garden produce is on display including the famous giant Haines strawberries developed by Charles Anway about 1900. Today this true

Left — Port Chilkoot, with the Chilkat Range looming in the background. (Pete Martin)

Alaskan hybrid is grown for export to all parts of the United States.

Another export item is lumber. For a number of years Haines relied on timber and its processing but ocean freighters loading lumber at Haines are no longer a familiar sight. One of the two sawmills closed permanently in October 1975, and the other operates only when enough logs are available.

Haines is most accessible by water as it is served regularly by the state ferries. A small airline offers scheduled flights to Juneau and Skagway. Haines and Hyder are the only Alaska Panhandle communities with direct interconnecting highway links to the Alaska Highway, and will remain so until the Skagway-Carcross Road is completed (in 1978, if on schedule).

On the highway, only 22 miles from Haines, is the Indian village of Klukwan, headquarters of the Chilkat tribe. It lies on the shore of a slow-moving, muddy river which crosses a wide, willow-fringed valley. As in most Native villages, the houses face the main avenue of transportation, and in Klukwan, they extend in a long line parallel to the Chilkat River.

Klukwan is known chiefly for its famous Chilkat blankets, or dance robes, woven from the long hair of mountain goats and from cedar bark fibers. A new tribal house was constructed in 1969, and it is the center of

174

community activities. This tribe has fostered the revival of Chilkat dances and tribal arts at the Chilkat Center for the Arts at Port Chilkoot.

Klukwan is also the site of one of the largest, richest magnetite, or iron, deposits in the world, which may be developed in the not-distant future by Japanese interests.

From late October through early February, thousands of bald eagles congregate along a 2-mile stretch of the Chilkat River near Klukwan to feed on spawned-out remains of a late salmon run. A warm current flowing from Big Salmon River keeps this stretch of the Chilkat River open most of the winter.

The annual gathering of approximately 3,500 eagles, believed to be from the Yukon Territory, Southeastern Alaska and British Columbia, is the largest in the world. Occasionally crowded like flocks of giant sparrows into cottonwood trees bordering the river, the eagles are easily visible from the Haines Highway, Miles 19 to 21.

In 1972 the Alaska State Legislature declared 4,800 acres of the Chilkat River Valley a Critical Habitat Area, which means any management of the area must not harm the eagle populations. The area is also under study as a potential Alaska state park, although the proposal has generated local controversy due to possible impediment of mining of the nearby iron ore deposits.

Left — **Haines is well known for its concentrations of eagles, which gather from late October through early February along a stretch of the Chilkat River, near Klukwan, to feed on spawned-out salmon. (Charlie Ott)**
Below — **One of the area's bald eagles surveys his domain. (Mark Kelley)**
Lower left — **Mountain goat hair and cedar bark fibers were used to make Chilkat blankets in Klukwan. This blanket, woven a few years ago in Sitka, is on display at Sitka National Historical Park. (Tim Thompson)**

Skagway

Boardwalks and weather-beaten buildings with false fronts line the main street of Skagway, one-time gateway to the Klondike gold rush. During its heyday Skagway had a floating population of up to 20,000. (Official 1977 population was 858.)

When the first stampeders landed at what is today Skagway, they overran the homestead of William Moore, who had settled there in 1888 after discovering the White Pass route through the Coast Mountains. A tent and shack city grew overnight as the hordes disembarked from steamers outbound from Pacific Northwest ports. All through the autumn of 1897 and into the winter, steamers continued to disgorge stampeders, cattle, horses, tools, food and villains. Numerous frame buildings, stores, saloons, gambling houses and dance halls lined the streets.

In the confusion, law and order disappeared as prospectors tried to accumulate supplies and claw their way over the formidable mountain barrier. For a time Soapy Smith—gambler, con artist and sometimes bully—controlled the town, but his reign ended in a shootout in which both he and challenger Frank Reid were killed.

There were two routes from Skagway to Dawson—White Pass, where a railroad was built, and Chilkoot Pass.

Opposite page — Aerial view of Skagway, near the head of Taiya Inlet. Milky water is created by silt from the Taiya and Skagway rivers. (Rick Furniss)

Left — Modern-day stampeders, looking for recreation more than gold, hike over Chilkoot Pass from Dyea (near Skagway), to Bennett, British Columbia . . . and beyond. The trail is now part of Klondike Gold Rush National Historical Park. (Tom Bean)

Below — Downtown Skagway retains an early-day flavor; the onion-domed building is the Golden North Hotel, featuring antiques in every room. (Sharon Paul, Staff)

The most popular was the latter which started at Dyea, about 7 miles north of Skagway. There stampeders began the strenuous climb to the summit, and then an equally hazardous journey across a series of lakes and downriver to the Klondike gold fields.

Today the old Chilkoot Pass has become a popular hiking trail and part of the Klondike Gold Rush National Historical Park. This park, authorized by Congress in 1976, follows the agony and glory of the old Trail of '98 from Seattle to Skagway, where several buildings have been renovated, and over the Chilkoot and White passes. On the Yukon Territory side, the Canadian government has been preserving the historic town of Dawson, helping create an international park commemorating the gold rush.

177

The White Pass & Yukon Route train makes daily runs from Skagway, Alaska, to Whitehorse, Yukon Territory, over the old narrow-gauge tracks. In this photo the train rounds a bend near the summit of White Pass, with peaks of the Coast Mountains in the background. (Stephen Hilson)

One of Skagway's attractions, the Trail of '98 Museum (owned by the townspeople), is also the first granite building constructed in Alaska. Built by the Methodist Church in 1899-1900 as McCabe College, it was never used for a school, but through legal entanglements was sold to the federal government. For decades it was used as a federal court building. Today a wealth of historical material has been preserved and made available to the public.

Another collection of memorabilia is displayed at Soapy Smith's Parlor, and not far away a gold rush graveyard contains the graves of both Soapy Smith and Frank Reid. Dyea, where only vestiges of buildings remain, will eventually become a park as funds become available to the new Klondike Gold Rush National Historical Park.

With the gold rush came construction of the White Pass & Yukon Route railway. Michael Heney and a group of British financiers surveyed the White Pass between Skagway and Lake Bennett, and in 14 months built a narrow-gauge line, which took miners and supplies beyond the summit to the Klondike.

The railroad and Skagway's unique geographic position secured its importance as a vital link between the sea and the Interior. Today the White Pass & Yukon Route has two docks along

the waterfront and provides daily passenger service to Whitehorse, Yukon Territory. A popular 1-day tour for visitors is to ride the vintage coach cars from Skagway to Lake Bennett, enjoy a hearty lunch and return over the pass to Skagway in the afternoon.

But freight is the year-round business of the railroad. It hauls lead-zinc concentrates from Anvil Mines, northwest of Whitehorse; asbestos from the Cassiar; lead-silver-zinc concentrates from Keno Hills mines; and copper ore from Whitehorse Copper Mines.

Another link with the Interior is the road between Skagway and Carcross, Yukon Territory, due for completion in 1978. Yukon highways (including the Alaska Highway) connect with Carcross, providing an alternative route to the Interior.

179

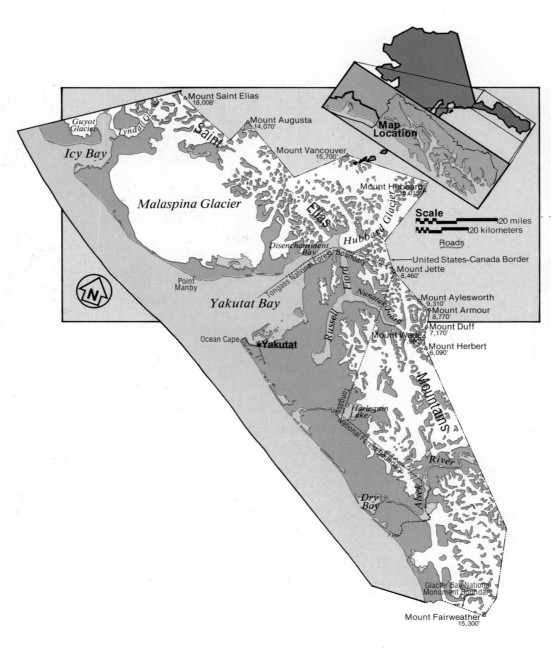

Map Location

Mount Saint Elias
18,008'

Guyot Glacier

Tyndall Glacier

Saint

Mount Augusta
14,070'

Icy Bay

Mount Vancouver
15,700'

Malaspina Glacier

Elias

Mount Hubbard
15,015'

Hubbard Glacier

Scale

20 miles
20 kilometers

Roads

Disenchantment Bay

Tongass National Forest Boundary

United States-Canada Border

Mount Jette
8,460'

Point Manby

Russell Fiord

Nunatak Fiord

Mount Aylesworth
9,310'
Mount Armour
8,770'

Yakutat Bay

Mount Duff
7,170'
Mount Wade
7,900'
Mount Herbert
6,090'

Ocean Cape

Yakutat

Tongass National Forest Boundary

Harlequin Lake

Mountains

River

Dry Bay

Alsek River

Glacier Bay National Monument Boundary

Mount Fairweather
15,300'

N

THE NORTHERN PANHANDLE

This is Southeastern Alaska's most remote corner, extending north from the boundary of Glacier Bay National Monument to Icy Bay and including the western slopes of the Saint Elias Mountains, Dry Bay, Yakutat Bay and the town of Yakutat, Russell Fiord, Mount Saint Elias and several major glaciers — notably Malaspina Glacier, largest on the North American continent.

Relatively few Alaskans have visited this region — except perhaps to stop briefly at Yakutat, which has daily jetliner connections with Anchorage, Juneau and other points.

Yakutat

Along the Gulf Coast of Alaska is a narrow neck of land connecting Southeastern to the main body of Alaska. On this great arc of the gulf there are few offshore islands and the surf, often driven by 100-mile-an-hour winds, pounds relentlessly on exposed beaches. One of the only refuges for vessels is Yakutat Bay. Yakutat, principal winter village of the Yakutat tribe of Tlingits, is just inside the mouth of this large bay.

The history of Yakutat began in pre-Russian days with the migration of Interior tribes and the northward expansion of the Tlingits.

Then came the white man in the 18th century. Both French explorer La Perouse and English Captain George Dixon stopped at Yakutat Bay in 1786; they were followed by Russian and Spanish explorers, and soon the region's sea otter pelts became a drawing card for Russian, Yankee and English fur traders.

Gold, in addition to the fur trade, left its mark when in 1887 black sand beaches in the area were being worked, producing up to $40 a ton. But a combination of disasters (including a tidal wave) stripped the sands of most of the gold before the miners could retrieve it.

Salmon bolstered Yakutat's economy during the first decades of the 20th century as the Gulf Coast offered some of the richest commercial salmon fishing in the region.

To process these fish, the first cannery was built in 1904 by a company with the unlikely name of Yakutat and Southern Railroad. The company actually built what was Southeastern's first standard-gauge rail line. It was used initially to haul timber to a company sawmill that supplied lumber for construction of a cannery, wharves and associated buildings. Later the railroad

Left — **Yakutat clings to the bluffs above Monti Bay. The green-roofed building on the right is a former cannery. (Rick Furniss)**
Above — **White water on Canada's Tatshenshini River, which joins the Alsek River about 50 miles inland from Dry Bay. The river was first explored by Edward James Glave and Jack Dalton (of Dalton Trail fame) in 1890. (Tim Thompson)**

Below — **Shore birds crowd the waters of Yakutat Bay and Monti Bay. Here a wandering tattler pokes among the rocks for small worms and other invertebrates. (Penny Rennick, Staff)**

Right — **Storm-tossed logs along a Yakutat beach. On sunny days a few hardy residents will brave the icy water of the Pacific for a quick swim. (Rick Furniss, reprinted from** *ALASKA GEOGRAPHIC*®**)**

ran 10 miles to the Situk and Lost rivers, where many fishermen set nets to capture the returning salmon. The fish were unloaded into gondola cars at certain points along the track and hauled to the cannery. But, since departures were determined by the rise and fall of the tide, its schedule was quite unlike any other railroad's.

Like most other salmon processors in Southeastern, the cannery closed when the salmon streams were fished out. Several floating canneries and smaller canning and cold-storage companies operated in season, but the community has suffered economically for years from the seasonal cycle of fishing employment. In recent years, sports fishing and hunting have attracted many visitors to the area, and tourism is likely to increase as a source of income. But it, too, is a seasonal activity.

Today about 450 people live in the Yakutat area—most of whom are Tlingits. There are modest hotels, restaurants, a lodge and basic businesses common to most small towns. Daily jet flights, north and south, are the primary means of access to Yakutat, as it is not serviced by the ferry system. Barge service is steady only during the summer.

All of this may change. If the prospect of offshore oil and gas development materializes, an influx of several thousand new people is possible.

In the fall of 1974 a consortium of three companies, Shell, ARCO and Mobil, purchased property near Yakutat for an industrial park to serve as a supply and operational base for their petroleum exploration activities in the gulf. Concern has been expressed by some Yakutat residents who wish to maintain a small-town lifestyle and continue to have subsistence use of natural resources.

Traditionally the people of Yakutat survived and prospered on fishing and hunting with logging as a much later addition. The transition from a fishing and recreational community to an industrial community potentially several times the present size involves more than a surface change in traditional lifestyles and character of the community. Consequently, Yakutat is trying to proceed with caution—planning each forward step with the involvement of local people, the oil industry and various state and federal agencies.

The hope in Yakutat—as in other modern Southeastern Alaska towns and villages—is to somehow avoid the boom-to-bust pattern that has been so common during past rushes . . . for gold, fur and fish.

Left — **Dense forests along Ocean Cape on the southeast tip of Yakutat Bay. (Rick Furniss, reprinted from** *ALASKA GEOGRAPHIC®***)**

183

A salmon seiner on its way
out of Yakutat Bay passes beneath
18,008-foot Mount Saint Elias.
(Rick Furniss, reprinted from
ALASKA GEOGRAPHIC®)

184

Left — Yakutat Bay, 15 nautical miles across at its opening, winds it way into the Saint Elias Mountains. (William Boehm)
Below — Hubbard Glacier, at the entrance to Russell Fiord. The ice pinnacle on the left calved shortly after this photo was taken. (Dr. W. S. Reeburgh, reprinted from *ALASKA®* magazine)

Far left — Massive Malaspina Glacier, with its gigantic folded moraines, is larger than Rhode Island and extends nearly 50 miles along the Pacific coast. (William Boehm)

Left — Icy Bay, at the northern edge of the Panhandle, extends 16 miles from the end of Guyot and Malaspina glaciers to the Pacific. (USGS photo by Donald Grybeck)

Islands Of Southeastern Alaska

In Order of Size
(Compiled by U.S. Forest Service)

Rank	Name	Acres	Square Miles	Miles of Coast	Rank	Name	Acres	Square Miles	Miles of Coast
1	Prince of Wales	1,427,659	2,231	990.1	35	Farm	8,928	13	19.0
2	Chichagof	1,346,463	2,104	742.0	36	Halleck	8,928	13	14.2
3	Admiralty	1,064,960	1,664	577.7	37	Brownson	8,340	13	19.8
4	Baranof	1,028,604	1,607	616.9	38	Deer	8,290	12	20.5
5	Revillagigedo	747,307	1,168	309.0	39	Partofshikof	8,290	12	16.8
6	Kupreanof	697,321	1,089	312.8	40	Dry	7,652	11	16.8
7	Kuiu	477,668	745	431.7	41	Thorne	7,652	11	15.8
8	Etolin	219,741	343	127.76	42	Krestof	7,015	10	23.1
9	Dall	162,639	254	218.0	43	Lemesurier	6,946	10	15.87
10	Wrangell	140,612	220	88.5	44	Fillmore	6,672	10	14.7
11	Mitkof	135,192	211	85.3	45	Tiedeman	6,272	9	22.1
12	Kosciusko	119,157	186	106.4	46	Orr	5,838	9	22.0
13	Zarembo	116,698	182	56.9	47	Marble	5,838	9	14.7
14	Kruzof	110,321	172	88.5	48	San Juan Bautista	5,838	9	11.4
15	Annette	86,741	130	89.9	49	Moser	5,739	8	14.3
16	Gravina	57,549	89	71.2	50	Hassler	5,004	7	11.7
17	Douglas	50,059	78	42.1	51	Goat	4,170	6	18.4
18	Heceta	46,707	72	64.2	52	Betton	4,170	6	11.0
19	Yakobi	46,261	72	60.2	53	Mummy	4,170	6	11.0
20	Sukkwan	44,204	69	48.8	54	Swan	4,095	6	12.6
21	Duke	38,366	59	49.5	55	Inian	4,081	6	26.0
22	Suemez	37,532	58	48.9	56	Hamilton	3,869	5	11.7
23	Long	35,030	55	50.3	57	Shrubby	3,826	5	10.5
24	Baker	33,362	52	55.2	58	Onslow	3,336	5	11.7
25	Noyes	31,694	49	31.2	59	Smeaton	3,336	5	11.0
26	Coronation	22,519	35	38.5	60	Sitklan	3,336	5	10.1
27	San Fernando	21,685	33	25.7	61	Khantaak	3,276	5	16.0
28	Tuxekan	21,044	32	28.8	62	Stevenson	3,188	4	9.5
29	Catharine	18,349	28	23.9	63	Blashke	3,188	4	7.5
30	Lulu	14,896	23	—	64	Vank	2,941	4	8.5
31	Woronkofski	14,667	22	19.6	65	Knight	2,550	4	8.5
32	Bell	12,511	19	22.0	66	Forrester	2,502	3	11.0
33	Warren	12,511	19	18.4					
34	Woewodski	10,203	15	17.4		**Total**		**13,429**	**6,006.9**

Southeastern Town Populations

	1970 census	1977 estimate	Date of incorporation
Angoon	400	500	1963
Craig	272	467	1922
Elfin Cove	49	60	UN
Gustavus	64	91	UN
Haines	1,125	1,366	1910
Hoonah	748	1,000	1946
Hydaburg	214	384	1927
Hyder	49	80	UN
Juneau (city & borough)	13,556	19,193	1900
Kake	448	679	1952
Kasaan	30	38	1976
Ketchikan (city & borough)	10,041	11,490	1900
Klawock	213	281	1929
Klukwan	103	110	UN
Kupreanof	36	42	1975
Metlakatla	1,050	1,051	1944
Myers Chuck	37	59	UN
Pelican	113	169	1943
Petersburg	2,042	2,126	1910
Point Baker, Port Protection	-	77	UN
Port Alexander	-	51	1974
Saxman	135	272	1930
Sitka (city & borough)	6,109	7,100	1920
Skagway	675	858	1900
Tenakee Springs	86	109	1971
Thorne Bay	443	550	UN
Wrangell	2,029	3,152	1903
Yakutat	190	442	1948

Precipitation In Southeastern Towns

	Total rainfall	Total snowfall
Angoon	38	63
Craig	110	32
Gustavus	54	71
Haines	53	77
Hydaburg	116	54
Hyder	103	208
Juneau	91	94
Kake	57	44
Ketchikan	154	33
Little Port Walter	221	123
Metlakatla	118	43
Pelican	123	106
Petersburg	106	103
Sitka	97	50
Skagway	26	39
Wrangell	82	72
Yakutat	133	214

(From *Alaska Regional Profiles, Southeast Region*
published by the University of Alaska, Arctic Environmental
Information and Data Center)

Dates In Southeastern Alaska

1741	Bering discovers Alaska
1793	George Vancouver explores Portland Canal, Behm Canal and northward, proving that North America has no ocean passage to the East Coast
1794	Vancouver explores and maps the coast to Yakutat
1799	Baranof establishes the post known today as Old Sitka
1802	Tlingit Indians attack the Russians at Sitka
1804	Founding of Sitka or Fort Archangel Michael
1861	Gold is discovered on the Stikine River
1867	Russia sells Alaska to the United States; Charles Sumner proposes the name "Alaska"
1868	The Customs Act passes; first bill related to Alaska
1876	Gold is discovered at Windham Bay near Juneau
1877	U.S. Army troops withdrawn from Alaska
1878	First commercial salmon canneries in Alaska built at Klawock and near Sitka
1880	Gold is discovered on Gastineau Channel; Juneau founded
1884	The First Organic Act passes Congress, creating a civil and judicial district; John H. Kinkead becomes Alaska's first governor, stationed in Sitka
1892	The first salmon hatchery in Southeastern started on Kuiu Island
1897	Start of the Klondike gold rush
1900	Civil Code for Alaska; Sitka becomes a judicial district, and Juneau becomes capital of the territory
1902	First cold-storage plant for freezing fish operates at Taku Harbor
1905	Alaska's first copper smelter built at Coppermount, Prince of Wales Island
1906	Capital moves to Juneau; Wilford B. Hoggatt is the first governor to live in the new seat of government
1907	Tongass National Forest, largest U.S. National Forest, is created by presidential proclamation
1912	Home Rule Act provides for a Territorial Legislature
1913	First Territorial Legislature meets in Juneau
1921	First pulp mill is established at Speel River, Port Snettisham
1958	Statehood Bill for Alaska is signed by President Eisenhower
1959	Statehood is proclaimed
1971	Alaska Native Claims Settlement Act passes

Coming attractions

BRISTOL BAY

The upcoming edition of *ALASKA GEOGRAPHIC*® (Volume 5, Number 3) will take readers to the fascinating Bristol Bay region — a large and surprising corner of Alaska where contradictions abound. (Bristol Bay's fishing grounds are well-known to many, but inland are wilderness areas still poorly charted. The region is one of the richest in the state in terms of natural resources — especially salmon — and among the poorest when it comes to amenities.)
Clockwise from top — Old Bristol Bay gill-netters sail across the bay. (Charlie Kroll) / Walrus on one of the Bay's remote islands. (Rollie Ostermick) / Hanging red salmon to dry at the village of Togiak. (Neil and Betty Johannsen)

STATEMENT OF OWNERSHIP MANAGEMENT and CIRCULATION

(Required by 39 U.S.C. 3685) ALASKA GEOGRAPHIC® is a quarterly publication, home offices, Box 4-EEE, Anchorage, Alaska 99509. Editor is Robert A. Henning. Publisher is The Alaska Geographic Society, Box 4-EEE, Anchorage, Alaska 99509. Owner is Alaska Northwest Publishing Co., Box 4-EEE, Anchorage, Alaska 99509. Robert A. Henning and Phyllis Henning, husband and wife, are owners of 97 percent of all common stock outstanding.

ALASKA GEOGRAPHIC® has a paid circulation of 9,209 subscribers and newsstand buyers.

I certify that statements above are correct and complete:

ROBERT A. HENNING
Editor

Alaska Geographic. Back Issues

Single copies of the *ALASKA GEOGRAPHIC*® back issues are also available. When ordering, please add $.50 postage/handling per copy.

The North Slope, Vol. 1, No. 1. Charter issue of *ALASKA GEOGRAPHIC*®. Out of print.

One Man's Wilderness, Vol. 1, No. 2. The story of a dream shared by many, fulfilled by few: a man goes into the bush, builds a cabin and shares his incredible wilderness experience. Color photos. 116 pages, $7.95

Admiralty . . . Island in Contention, Vol. 1, No. 3. An intimate and multifaceted view of Admiralty: its geological and historical past, its present-day geography, wildlife and sparse human population. Discusses the views of factions "in contention" for the island. Color photos. 78 pages, $5.00

Fisheries of the North Pacific: History, Species, Gear & Processes, Vol. 1, No. 4. Out of print.

The Alaska-Yukon Wild Flowers Guide, Vol. 2, No. 1. First Northland flower book with both large, color photos and detailed drawings of every species described. Features 160 species from every geographic area of Alaska and the Yukon. Common and scientific names, plus maximum growing height. 112 pages, $7.95

Richard Harrington's Yukon, Vol. 2, No. 2. A collection of 277 stunning color photos by Canadian photographer-writer Richard Harrington captures the Yukon in all its seasons and moods, from Watson Lake to Herschel Island. 103 pages, $7.95

Prince William Sound, Vol. 2, No. 3. Out of print.

Yakutat: The Turbulent Crescent, Vol. 2, No. 4. Out of print.

Glacier Bay: Old Ice, New Land, Vol. 3, No. 1. The expansive wilderness of Southeastern Alaska's Glacier Bay National Monument unfolds in crisp text and color photographs. Records the flora and fauna of the area, its natural history, with hike and cruise information, plus a large-scale color map. 132 pages, $9.95

The Land: Eye of the Storm, Vol. 3, No. 2. Out of print.

Richard Harrington's Antarctic, Vol. 3, No. 3. The Canadian photojournalist guides readers through remote and little understood regions of the Antarctic and Subantarctic. More than 200 color photos and a large fold-out map. 104 pages, $8.95

The Silver Years of the Alaska Canned Salmon Industry: An Album of Historical Photos, Vol. 3, No. 4. Commemorates a boom or bust era in Alaska's romantic history, and more than 293 photos record the history of the industry — late 19th century to the present. Text links the photographs by subject — canneries, boats and gear, transportation. 168 pages, $7.95

Alaska's Volcanoes: Northern Link in the Ring of Fire, Vol. 4, No. 1. Scientific overview supplemented with eyewitness accounts of Alaska's historic volcano eruptions. Includes color and black-and-white photos and a schematic description of the effects of plate movement upon volcanic activity. 88 pages, $7.95

The Brooks Range: Environmental Watershed, Vol. 4, No. 2. Looks at early exploration and at controversy over uses for the region: Native land claims, recreation, proposed national parks and development of resources. Maps, color photos. 112 pages, $9.95

Kodiak: Island of Change, Vol. 4, No. 3. Although half the size of New Jersey, and once the administrative center of Russian Alaska, the 3,588-square-mile island of Kodiak remains well off the beaten path. Past, present and future — everything from Russian exploration to the present-day quest for oil. Maps, color photos. 96 pages, $7.95

Wilderness Proposals: Which Way for Alaska's Lands?, Vol. 4, No. 4. Out of print.

Cook Inlet Country, Vol. 5, No. 1. A visual tour of the region — its communities, big and small, and its countryside. Begins at the southern tip of the Kenai Peninsula, circles Turnagain Arm and Knik Arm for a close-up view of Anchorage, and visits the Matanuska and Susitna valleys and the wild, west side of the inlet. 144 pages; 230 color photos, separate map. $9.95

FORTHCOMING ISSUES:

Bristol Bay Basin, Vol. 5, No. 3. Explores this land of contradictions and change; illustrated with contemporary color photos and historic black-and-whites; fold-out map. $9.95

Alaska Whales and Whaling, Vol. 5, No. 4. The wonders of whales in Alaska are explored through color photos, illustrations, historic photos and text; poster of 14 whale illustrations by Don Sineti. $9.95

Yukon-Kuskokwim Delta, Vol. 6, No. 1. Studies the sprawling lowland where the great Yukon and Kuskokwim rivers meet the Bering Sea; the homeland of the Yup'ik Eskimo whose lives are a unique blend of ancestral and modern lifestyles. Numerous color black-and-white photos; fold-out map. $9.95

Your $20 membership in The Alaska Geographic Society includes 4 subsequent issues of *ALASKA GEOGRAPHIC*®, the Society's official quarterly. Please add $1 for non-U.S. membership.
Additional membership information available upon request. To order back issues send your check or money order and volumes desired to:

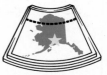

The Alaska Geographic Society

Box 4-EEE, Dept. AGS, Anchorage, AK 99509